are ready to take control of your financial destiny, you would be well advised to **READ THIS BOOK**."

LAURA TARBOX, CFP
Tarbox Equity

"Mary Rowland is well known to the public and professionals alike for addressing financial planning issues in an **ACCURATE, DETAILED, AND READABLE STYLE**. This is not just a 'how-to' book. Rather, Rowland makes practical suggestions for the investment portfolio that provide **A THOUGHTFUL ROAD MAP** through the retirement planning maze."

MICHAEL J. CHASNOFF, CFP
President, Advanced Capital Strategies

"**A REFRESHING BREAK** from the feel-bad books about life after work, and **A STERLING RESOURCE** that shows the difference between planning for retirement and merely saving."

DAVID ALBERTSON
Editor, *Employee Benefit News*

"Wow! If the key to success is under-promising and over-delivering, this mildly labeled book fits the bill! Not only does the reader learn all the ins and outs of 401(k) investing, in the process he or she gets a world of information about investing in general and life planning. Mary Rowland has done her research well, and she communicates it with **REAL-LIFE EXAMPLES** to bring the message into focus. **A GOOD ADDITION TO ANYONE'S FINANCIAL LIBRARY**."

ROBERT E. WACKER, CFP, EA
R. E. Wacker Associates

A
COMMONSENSE
GUIDE TO YOUR
401(k)

MARY ROWLAND

Also available from
THE BLOOMBERG PERSONAL BOOKSHELF

Smarter Insurance Solutions
by Janet Bamford

Smart Questions to Ask Your Financial Advisers
by Lynn Brenner

Investing in Small-Cap Stocks
by Christopher Graja and
Elizabeth Ungar, Ph.D.

A Commonsense Guide to Mutual Funds
by Mary Rowland

Choosing and Using an HMO
by Ellyn Spragins

And from
THE BLOOMBERG PROFESSIONAL LIBRARY

Best Practices for Financial Advisors
by Mary Rowland

Protecting Your Practice
by Katherine Vessenes
in cooperation with the International
Association for Financial Planning

BLOOMBERG PERSONAL BOOKSHELF

A
COMMONSENSE
GUIDE TO YOUR

401(k)

MARY ROWLAND

BLOOMBERG PRESS
PRINCETON

Books are available for bulk purchases at special discounts. Special editions or book excerpts can also be created to specifications. For information, please write: Special Markets Department, Bloomberg Press.

This publication contains the author's opinions and is designed to provide accurate and authoritative information. It is sold with the understanding that the author, publisher, and Bloomberg L.P. are not engaged in rendering legal, accounting, investment-planning, or other professional advice. The reader should seek the services of a qualified professional for such advice; the author, publisher, and Bloomberg L.P. cannot be held responsible for any loss incurred as a result of specific investments or planning decisions made by the reader.

First edition published 1998
1 3 5 7 9 10 8 6 4 2

Rowland, Mary

    A commonsense guide to your 401(k) / Mary Rowland.

      p.   cm. – (The Bloomberg personal bookshelf)

    ISBN 1-57660-019-X

    1. 401(k) plans. 2. 401(k) plans—Law and legislation—United States. 3. Pension trusts—Law and legislation—United States.

    I. Title. II. Series.

    HD7105.45.U6R68   1997

    332.024'01—dc21   97-35143

                                                      CIP

Pie charts by Myra Klockenbrink

Acquired and edited by Christine Miles

Book design by Don Morris Design

To my mom

— M . R .

PART 7

403(b)s, 457 Plans, Etc.   **226**

PART 8

Sample Portfolios
*A top-notch financial planner clarifies the
risks and rewards of these 14 examples*   **242**

RESOURCES   **256**

INTRODUCTION

HIS IS A BOOK about how to squeeze the most value out of your 401(k) plan. But it has ambitions of going beyond that; of helping you to think about how to use your capital to create the life you want for yourself—along the way, as well as in retirement. To do that, you must do more than just contribute to your 401(k) plan and invest wisely. You need to do some serious thinking about where you are going in your career and in your life and how your 401(k) plan might help you get there. You may even need to think a little bit about where the 401(k) plan came from, why it has grown, and what that means for you both today and later in your nonworking years.

In March 1997, *The New York Times* ran an article about the resilient economic expansion of the 1990s—six years old and still vibrant. But the story of that economic expansion certainly has not been one of prosperity for all Americans. The expansion masks a lot of pain. Thousands of workers might legitimately feel that this period of economic growth was built on their broken backs. Behind the story of growth is the story of the severed employment contract. Gone is the promise that if you work hard, your employer will take care of you both as a worker and as a retiree.

That's because part of the price of the expansion was a massive corporate restructuring that forced millions of people out of work and into lesser jobs. Indeed, the *Times* reported that 13 million people—or 10 percent of the work force—are now temporary or contract workers. These people have no employee benefits, which makes them a much cheaper source of labor for employers. And they provide a vast pool of "just-in-time labor," holding down wages for others who do hold jobs. Of course, not all of these contract workers are unhappy about their lot. Many of them see self employment as the answer to a prayer. These are the lucky ones.

The 401(k) plan is a small but important part of this change in corporate America. What you do with it depends on whether you view this glass as half empty or half full.

This is not a self-help book. I'm not going to talk about the power of positive thinking or lecture you about paying yourself first. Still, I can't resist urging you to make the most of the tools that are available to you. Inasmuch as you can view the revolution in the American workplace as an opportunity for you to create independence for yourself rather than seeing it as a cause for disappointment, you will certainly have a better work life and a better retirement life. The 401(k) plan can play a key role in helping you to do that.

To understand the role this plan plays in

modern corporate America, I think it's important to take a look at its roots. Having been a history major in college, I always feel that if we can understand the origin of something, we can deal with it better. And in this case, it is actually a fascinating story of how one person helped shape the most vital savings tool many Americans have today.

Congress added paragraph k to section 401 of the Internal Revenue Code as part of the Revenue Act of 1978. But that paragraph *could* have gone entirely unnoticed. It simply permitted companies to set up tax-deferred savings plans so long as the plans didn't unduly favor the top-earning one-third of the company's employees. In other words, it provided for a "discrimination test." If an employee benefit is to receive a tax advantage, it must be offered (and used by) employees at various income levels. This paragraph said that deferred savings plans must pass that test. Nothing too remarkable about that.

There was a reason for addressing this issue in the first place, though. Paragraph k was actually written to resolve a conflict over cash profit-sharing plans that were prevalent among major companies in the early 1970s. Many companies had replaced year-end cash bonuses with plans that allowed employees to set aside a portion of the bonus in a tax-deferred account.

Tax-deferral is always more appealing to those who make more money and pay more tax. (At the time, we had a series of different tax rates that peaked out at 70 percent.) Lower-paid workers are less likely to opt for tax deferral. They pay less tax and they have less money to stretch to meet their needs. Suppose a bank teller typically received an $800 bonus at Christmas time. Under the bank profit-sharing plans of the early 1970s, half of that would go into the retirement plan and the teller could choose whether to defer the other half as well or to take that $400 in cash. This hybrid plan also typically allowed employees to withdraw money from the retirement plan after two years.

Although all workers had the same options, they didn't make the same choices. The higher-paid workers chose to defer their entire bonus while lower-paid workers typically chose half cash and then pulled the rest of the money out as soon as possible. The government objected to this arrangement because the tax benefit was really going to the higher-paid employees. The fact that everybody had the same opportunity was immaterial, from the government's point of view.

In 1972, the Internal Revenue Service ruled that no new hybrid bonus plans like these could be set up. Two years later, the Employee Retirement Income Security Act, or ERISA, was passed. ERISA was landmark legislation, providing a massive body of rules and regulations to govern private pension plans and to protect the participants in them. When ERISA was passed, Congress said that it would make a ruling on the hybrid plans. That happened in 1978 when paragraph k was written, stipulating that the plans could continue, but only if they didn't favor the top one-third of employees. Paragraph k took effect in January 1980.

Like other benefits consultants, R. Theodore Benna read paragraph k carefully. Even though it presented nothing really new, it was his business and he had to pay attention. "The myth was that nobody knew it was there," Benna says now. "But that wasn't true. I studied it, and so did anyone else who follows this section of the law." But no one saw it as particularly significant. "January came and went, and nobody was doing anything," Benna says. But Benna didn't drop it. He was working with a bank that wanted to revamp its traditional defined benefit pension plan and eliminate an old cash bonus plan. (Defined benefit plans get their name because the plan "defines" the benefit you will receive in retirement. Funding the plan and paying out the

benefit are the responsibilities of the employer.
Benefits are calculated based on salary and years
of service with a company.)

It was clear to Benna that section 401's
paragraph k would permit his bank client to
replace the cash bonus plan with a deferred
profit-sharing plan, provided the new plan
included lower-paid workers so that it would meet
the discrimination test. But Benna didn't think
lower-paid workers would participate. If they did
not, the plan wouldn't pass the test and it would
not be permitted. "I'd worked with employees
long enough to know that the bulk of them
wouldn't be willing to set aside a big chunk of
pay for retirement just to save money in taxes,"
Benna says.

So Benna began to study paragraph k to see
how he might interpret it to help his client
include lower-paid workers in the retirement plan
so that it would pass the test. He came up with
two key concepts that made the 401(k) plan what

it is today: He saw that the savings could come from regular salary rather than bonuses, and he came up with the idea of deducting contributions on a regular basis from each employee paycheck. More importantly, he developed the concept of employer matching funds, the key to the attractiveness of the 401(k) plans. "Neither of these was in the code," Benna says. "But I took the position that if something wasn't prohibited, you could do it."

As it turned out, his bank client didn't want to be a guinea pig and test an interpretation of the new law that hadn't been specifically laid out. So Benna's own employer, the Johnson Companies, set up the first 401(k) savings plan on January 1, 1981, as a test case. In November of that year, the Internal Revenue Service acknowledged that Benna's interpretation of paragraph k was an acceptable one.

The 401(k) plan took off almost immediately for one key reason: It allowed employers to begin shifting the immense responsibility for retirement saving to their employees. Critics see this as evil. Few of us can view the changes in corporate America over the last two decades without emotion because few of us have been untouched. But from a bird's eye view it was more pragmatic than evil. American companies were beginning to feel the heat of intense global competition. For many of them it was cut costs or perish. Some of them may have done it heartlessly. But it is clear that corporations needed to do what they could to cut costs. We all live with the mixed results: A bull market in stocks that roared on seemingly endlessly combined with uncertain employment prospects for Americans at every stage in their career, from those just out of college to those approaching retirement. Today more than 22 million Americans participate in 401(k) plans, which now have assets of around $750 billion. And the plans are, in fact, the best investment around for employees who have the opportunity to use them.

One troubling aspect of this is that with the millions of dollars corporations have spent to convince employees that 401(k) plans are wonderful, there is no one spending an equivalent amount of money to look for the negatives. In fact, 401(k) plans are in a somewhat unique position of having no real detractors. During the first 15 years of their existence, nary a negative word was heard about them. The business press couldn't say enough good things about them, and the line between business reporters and company publicists was blurred in an interesting way, too. Because companies are required to communicate to employees about 401(k) plans, many teamed up with journalists who wrote books and newsletters that presented the company point of view in a subtle way. One good example is *Money* magazine's newsletter, *Managing Your Future,* which goes to about 1 million plan participants from a number of different companies. These companies pay to produce and distribute the newsletter to their employees. The *Money* name implies that it is a journalistic endeavor. But it's highly doubtful that a book or newsletter endorsed and circulated by an employer that sponsors a plan will raise controversial issues about these plans.

One result of all this coziness is that there has not been enough objective criticism of 401(k) plans. And the plans have gotten increasingly expensive: Costs are going up, not down. "We keep hearing that the 401(k) marketplace is so competitive," says Lynn Brenner, author of *Building Your Nest Egg With Your 401(k)* (1995, Investors Press Inc.), and the 401(k) columnist for *Bloomberg Personal.* "That competition is certainly doing nothing to force fees down." Brenner says that's because sponsors are passing those costs on and participants haven't noticed yet. But she predicts that will change. "Most reporters—me included—have been telling employees for years that 401(k) plans are the best thing since sliced bread. For the next several years, you will be reading in the press about what is wrong with 401(k) plans. And it will start with how much they cost," Brenner says. Indeed, in its April 1997 issue, *Money* magazine blasted 401(k) expenses as "The Great Retirement Ripoff." I also wrote a piece, for the September 1997 issue of *Bloomberg Personal,* called "Your 401(k)'s Dirty Little Secret." Stay tuned on this issue.

There has been little constructive criticism about the investment options that employer sponsors offer, either. Some companies—like Bloomberg—offer choices that are too conservative and too limited. Others—General Motors is a notable example—offer too many choices for most employees to whittle down. And most sponsors don't do a very good job of helping employees make investment decisions. None of this is a reason to avoid the plan. But it does mean that you need to look beyond what your plan sponsor is offering in the way of education about the plan.

As for Ted Benna, his brainchild certainly didn't make him a rich man. Indeed, his career mirrors that of tens of thousands of men and women in the years since the 401(k) was developed. His employer was purchased by another benefits consultant, and then another. Benna worked on a contract until it ran out in 1993, when he was just 52. But Benna had been a partner at Johnson Companies and he was financially able to choose what he wanted to do. He didn't want to retire. Yet he needed a job that would accommodate his considerable volunteer work. A deeply religious man, he sits on the boards of a seminary, a bible college, and a church, and he speaks regularly to a group of Christian businessmen.

He also wanted to do something that would increase retirement savings for rank-and-file employees rather than for the high-paid executives who hired him as an employee benefits consultant. "Most of my work up until that point had been for small-business owners and professionals," Benna says. "There was a great tendency for these people to want to get personal benefit from their companies' retirement plans and to give very little to employees." During his consultant years, it was his job to satisfy clients. "I was good at the game. But after being involved in that business for a while, I really lost my appetite for it," he says.

So Benna went out on his own, setting up the 401(k) Association, whose mission he defines as "anything that would fall under protecting and promoting 401(k) plans." Benna believes 401(k)s are politically vulnerable because they cost so much in lost tax revenues and because they don't have a special lobbying group. The members of his group, who pay a small annual fee, are mostly individual plan participants who want to keep abreast of changes in this area. But Benna also sets up 401(k) plans for very small businesses at a nominal cost—his way, he says, of giving back and helping those who really need the retirement plans.

Benna's choices reflect those that most of us must make, and inasmuch as we can anticipate them and be ready, we will undoubtedly be more satisfied. The 401(k) is part of the employment landscape today. It is important for you to be able to look at that in an objective way. In the years since these plans were introduced, they have come to dominate the world of personal finance and financial planning advice. Dozens of articles and books urge Americans to contribute, contribute, contribute to a 401(k) plan. There are studies done and articles written every day that show that Americans do not save enough for retirement. When you read these studies, you should remember that they are funded by vendors like Merrill Lynch and Fidelity Investments who have a huge stake in 401(k) plans: There are billions of dollars to be made from 401(k) plans.

That does not mean that what these studies say is not true. But they present a black-and-white picture that is discouraging to those who are struggling along in their lives trying to figure out how to pay the mortgage and wondering whether they will survive the next round of corporate downsizings. This book does not assume that a 401(k) will solve all your problems in life. Nor does it assume that saving for retirement is the only thing you have to do with your money. Instead it will try to convince you that you should aim for financial independence and tell you how to make your 401(k) part of that overall "freedom strategy." Perhaps you will not have the luxury of leaving the money in your plan until you retire. Perhaps you will not want to. But get it in there. That will increase your options.

In nearly 25 years of writing about business and money issues—six of them as the personal finance columnist for *The New York Times*—I've learned that for most Americans, dealing with money is more about psychology and less about dollars and cents. If you are told that you need $1 million worth of life insurance, $1 million in your retirement account, and $350,000 to educate your kids, you're likely to feel discouraged, throw up your hands, and give up on the whole matter of financial planning.

So rather than focusing on seemingly impossible goals, I think it's better for you to buy *some* life insurance, put *some* money in a retirement account, and think a bit about college saving. But you should understand that the money in your 401(k) can be an important tool for many things you hope to achieve in life. So I'm going to tell you that 401(k) plans are a terrific financial planning tool, that they should be your first priority for savings dollars, and give you some investment tips on how to get the most out of them. I'll also show you, of course, what you need for a comfortable retirement. But I'm not going to beat the drum for 200 pages on why you can never expect to do anything but be a wage slave. Instead, I want you to think about where you're going and how setting aside some tax-deferred money can help you get there.

I'm going to tell you, too, that the baby-boom generation will need to work longer than their parents did. Indeed, the retirement age for Social Security is already changing for that generation. How terrible, then, to think you must work longer in a job you detest.

Consider William M. Walters, the subject of a page-one story in *The Wall Street Journal* in the spring of 1997. Walters, who spends his work weeks lugging heavy boxes and delivering food for the Chattanooga, Tennessee, school district, is 73 years old. He earns $6 an hour. But Walters is not a man on the fringes of society. He is the backbone of middle America—one of those men and women who worked hard all their lives.

Walters farmed with his family, served in the Navy during World War II, and then landed a solid job as branch manager of an auto parts delivery company. He lived what many Americans think of as the good life, earning $500 a week when the average family income in Chattanooga was just one-third of that. He was able to buy a 16-foot power boat for water skiing, a camper truck, and a motor home for taking fishing vacations in Florida.

But in 1990, when he was 67 years old, his employer closed his division, and Walters was out of work. Like many small companies, his employer, American Battery Inc. of Nashville, had no pension plan. So Walters, who had no savings, received just $16,000 a year from Social Security to cover living expenses for himself and his 67-year-old wife, who suffers from emphysema. It was not enough. And Walters is forced to work 30 hours a week to bring in an extra $640 a month. In fact, the *Journal* reported, Walters is part of a reversal of the trend toward earlier retirement. For most of the 20th century, the percentage of older people in the workplace had been declining. But that trend reversed in 1985 when 10.4 percent of those 65 and older reported having jobs. In January 1997, that number had grown to 12.7 percent.

If we face a longer work life, it behooves us to fix it now. I was influenced in my thinking about retirement by some work I did recently with a group of financial planners. To report a book called *Best Practices for Financial Advisors* (Bloomberg Press, 1997), I did a series of conference calls with 55 top financial planners from all over the country. I got an inside look at the financial planning process and was able to see how the top advisers work with their clients. Two planners in particular come to mind for the point I am trying to make here. They are Cynthia Meyers in Sacramento, California, and George Kinder in Cambridge, Massachusetts.

Meyers and Kinder do what they call "lifetime planning." What they mean by that is that they look at all aspects of the client's life rather than just financial needs. "I think too much emphasis is placed on retirement planning to the exclusion of creating a happy life for yourself," says Kinder, a Harvard graduate who is also a certified public accountant. Is this heresy? No. And Kinder practices what he preaches. Some years ago, when he was in his early thirties, Kinder took the Hawaiian vacation he had been dreaming about. Maui was everything he had expected—and more. He discovered a different side of himself that he hadn't known existed in his buttoned-down life of the mind in Cambridge.

Kinder made spending more time in Hawaii a top financial-planning goal. He stretched out his annual vacations to three and then four weeks. That still didn't satisfy him. So in 1991 he set up a financial-planning practice in Maui and began spending six months of the year there and six in

Cambridge. Of course Kinder, who is 49, still saves for retirement. But he created the life for himself that he loves. He combined the practical, intellectual side of his life with his passion for the rain forests of Hawaii. And he used some of his capital to do it. Kinder probably won't mind working longer, when he can do it on his terms. We could all learn a lesson from him about taking the time and energy to pursue passion in our lives. It does not mean that we need not save for retirement. It means we need to develop a lifetime plan and include the transition to retirement as part of it.

I hope this book will set you thinking about how you might do that. It is a bit different in its organization. I have put together 92 short essays on steps you need to take to get the most from your 401(k). They cover everything from getting into the plan to getting out of it and maximizing your money in retirement. Although they move in a somewhat logical order, each thought is independent and presented on a single two-page spread. That means you can open the book anywhere and get one piece of information. You needn't read the book from front to back. You can dip in and read something you find interesting—or find something you need to know right now. It will not be the end of the work you need to do, either. Lifetime planning is a big job—and a critical one. Putting money in your 401(k) plan is an important way to get started.

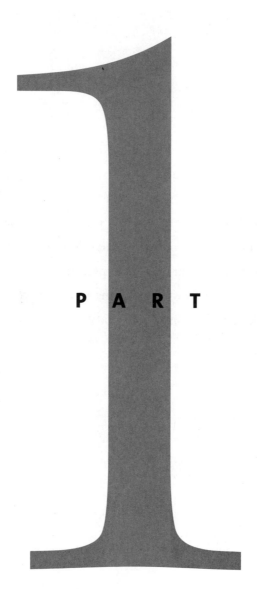

PART

1

The
Retirement
LANDSCAPE

HE OTHER DAY, a friend of mine was remembering his father, a hurried man who denied himself small pleasures to focus on the task at hand. The pleasures would come later, his father always said, when he retired. Then he would golf, fish, read, swim. He retired at 60 and moved from Chicago to Florida, where he built a house with a pool, bought golf clubs, fishing equipment—the works. You know the story. He didn't golf or fish or swim or read. He was bored to death. Fortunately, though, my friend's father saw that the Florida life was a mistake for him. He moved to the San Francisco Bay area, where he worked part time and puttered and tinkered the rest of the time for the remainder of his life.

Lest you think I'm opposed to relaxing and a promoter of workaholism, let me tell you another story. Stan Breitbard retired as national director of

Price Waterhouse in 1995 at the age of 56. Stan wanted a change and fully expected to find another full-time position somewhere near his home in Los Angeles. It didn't work out that way, though.

I was talking to Stan one day in the spring of 1997 about how retirement was going. He had developed a plan for teaching personal finance to students pursuing their master's degrees in business administration. He'd taught the course at Berkeley and loved doing it. He'd also joined a reading circle—he was the only man, he said— and was reading and discussing the classics as well as modern fiction. He also had plans to build on his lifelong passion for James Joyce by compiling a bibliography of works by and about the author and by forming a *Ulysses* reading group. And he was spending a great deal of time on the Internet, pursuing his interests in investing and financial planning.

But what about the second career? Well, Stan replied, it just wasn't appealing anymore. There were too many other things he wanted to do. Do you still need to do a financial plan—a career plan, a life plan—in retirement? I wanted to know. "Of course," Stan said. "I rethink what I'm doing constantly. I think about where I want to live, what I want to do, how I want to work."

My point is an obvious one. Your working life and your retirement life are not two distinct phases, one drudgery and one pleasure. Those who work successfully and retire successfully knit the two together, almost seamlessly. But it is not easy. It requires a great deal of thought—about who you are, what you want, what you enjoy, where you're going. And a great deal of planning. In a sense, this is the very toughest part of financial planning because it requires facing up to who you are and what you dream about. Top financial planners, like Stan Breitbard, say they have lost clients because they've asked them to face these questions.

Stan asked his MBA students at Berkeley to draw up a five-year financial plan for themselves. The students fell into three groups. The first concentrated on simple bookkeeping tasks: Paying off bills, developing a filing system, getting organized. The second group focused on saving and investing and some longer-term goals. But the third group looked at real financial planning—dreaming dreams and thinking about where they would go in life and how they would get there.

You wouldn't be reading a 401(k) book if you weren't thinking about your retirement—or perhaps worrying about your retirement. So much of what we read is designed to make us frightened that we won't have enough money to retire. When you think of retirement, I urge you to think of it in the broadest possible terms. Don't think of it as a compromise. Spin out all your dreams. Stretch to include everything in life that you might want to be. And then think about how you might accomplish it.

THINK ABOUT HOW
RETIREMENT IS CHANGING

STEP

1

Wherever you are in your working life, take a little time now to reflect on what you can expect from a job or career—and what you can expect later, when it's over. Twenty years from now—or even 10 years from now—work and retirement will not be such distinct phases of life as they are for today's retirees.

Work life in America was redefined in the 1980s and 1990s as more than 43 million jobs were erased, a number that comes from a *New York Times* analysis of U.S. Department of Labor statistics. Many new jobs appeared. But too many that were lost belonged to higher-paid, white-collar workers—those employees who looked forward to a pension and a comfortable retirement.

These middle managers were replaced by contract workers. "Consultant" is the euphemism for many of those who today earn low wages and receive no benefits. The *Times* told the story of Steven A. Holthausen, who was laid off from his $1,000-a-week job as a bank loan officer at age 50 and felt lucky to land a job dispensing tourist information off Interstate 95 in Connecticut.

This revolutionary change in the workplace will be followed by a revolutionary change in retirement. Certainly Holthausen does not expect a rich pension. This should not depress you. But it should make you think about what you will do with your work life and your nonwork life and how you might merge them together in a way that is satisfying for you. Charles Handy, a sometime professor and author on organizational change, made some suggestions in his book *The Age of Unreason* (Harvard Business School Press). When Handy wrote in 1990 that working at a corporation is no longer a viable alternative for most people, it seemed startling. Less than a decade later, it seems quite clear.

Handy, who began his career as an oil executive and then became a teacher and writer, predicted that workers in the 21st century will fit into one of three types: managers and technicians who will run the corporations; unskilled clerks and laborers; and creative people like consultants, designers, and others who work on a contract basis. Not only will many of us spend our working lives as self-employed contractors, Handy said, but all of us will work until a much later age. Even those managers and technicians who work as employees will remain in their jobs only until age 55 or so, he said, at which point they will have 15 or 20 more work years.

To prepare for this future, Handy recommends that you develop a portfolio of skills, services, and products that you can sell to corporations and to others in the marketplace. When his own two children left college, he told them: "I hope you won't look for a job in a corporation." Instead, he advised: "Look for customers. If you have a saleable skill, you can always work."

Handy's advice is right on target. Demographics play a role too. As we live longer—and enjoy better health—most of us will want to be productive. Whether you are just starting out in your career, you are at midpoint, or you are nearing the finish line, work on skills you need and develop the talents that you have. Retirement at age 55—or even 60 or 65— will no longer be an option for most people working today. Those who have a portfolio of skills will be able to pick and choose what they will do and when they want to do it. For them, a blend of work and leisure can be a pleasure. It will solve the problems of both work and retirement.

FOCUS ON WHAT
YOU DO WELL

STEP 2

Here is the problem for millions of middle managers who were "outplaced" or "downsized" over the past 15 years: They know how to manage people. But no one will pay them to do that anymore. As corporations have become flatter and team management has replaced the management hierarchy, few people are being paid simply to manage other people. If you want to succeed, you must identify something that you can do that commands a fee, or a salary.

It's not easy for many people to think of what their skills and talents are beyond the title a corporation has given them. "But we all have a lot of neglected talents," says Charles Handy. "It's a matter of redefining yourself. You need help because you've only seen yourself in one light."

To free up your thinking about what you're good at, Handy suggests that you go to 20 people you know and ask each to tell you one thing you do very well. Handy instructed a 48-year-old advertising executive who had just lost his job to do that exercise. "It was sort of embarrassing," this former adman told Handy. "I got 20 answers and not one of them was advertising." Instead, this man was told that he was very creative, good at organizing teams, presenting ideas, leading people, selecting wines, and recalling historical details. What to do with that?

This one-time adman set up a business taking people on tours of battlefields and other historical sights and vineyards throughout Europe. "He was able to redefine his whole life," Handy says. "It was a nice example of what you can do with some original thinking." It shows, too, that it pays to stretch far afield when you think about what you do well.

Consider, too, what outplacement firms do for those who are laid off—or what they used to do when employers allotted bigger budgets to this function. The first step might be to write an autobiography, breaking up your life into chapters: early childhood, grade school, high school, college, first job. When you get to career, think broadly of the tasks you have done rather than what you've been called. People tend to think of their career as their recent job. In fact, even if you have spent your career at one company, you have no doubt had several separate and distinct jobs. Think, too, of particular tasks that you have enjoyed and things you've done well—on the job, in school, or in volunteer projects.

When people go through this process, they often discover that there was one particular stop in their career where they loved what they were doing. As they moved along, that passion often got lost or misplaced as they became subsumed by corporate politics and the day-to-day demands of earning a living. Thinking through the process helps them rediscover what it was they really liked to do. That's why so many people who go through the painful layoff process later say, "It's the best thing that ever happened to me."

Even if you are happy in your job now, you need to hone your skills. And no matter what you do well—and what you end up doing—you will need some computer skills. If you have been procrastinating, get going. You need to know how to use the computer and how to find your way around the Internet. Learn what research tools are available and how specialists in your industry use the computer. Lack of familiarity with the computer labels you as a dinosaur. Develop your skills in writing, communications, foreign languages, and mathematics, too. These are skills that you will need in any business—and that will be handy if you work for yourself.

SET UP YOUR OWN SHOP

STEP
3

It doesn't have to be today, of course. But sometime in your career, you will work for yourself. Many people dream of owning their own business. Many others are terrified at the prospect. A decade ago the advice was this: Operating your own business requires a big appetite for risk, good organizational skills, rigid self-discipline, the ability to combat loneliness. If you don't have that skill set, you're an employee.

Forget that. Depending on a paycheck from a corporation is a luxury most Americans cannot afford anymore. Wherever you are in your work life, you should have an escape plan. You need a skill that someone will pay you for. The best way to find out what it is is to think about how you might set up an independent business. There is almost no job—from anesthesiology to zoology—that can't be done on a contract basis. And all kinds of people thrive as entrepreneurs. One of the most important tools you need is a passion for what you do.

Today many talented, entrepreneurial people move in and out of corporations. They develop their skills working for one or more employers and then set up their own shop—as a designer, consultant, writer, electrician, carpenter, software developer— and develop a roster of clients. Often they find that one client is consuming more and more time and providing more satisfying work. Perhaps they join that company as an employee.

But there are a couple of differences between this worker and the employee of the 1960s. First, our modern worker has a skill set that is portable. Second, he never becomes lulled into thinking the corporation will take care of him. That notion is ancient history. Workers in the 21st century will need to focus on their own skills and how to develop them rather than on corporate politics and how to stay on the right side of the boss. You should always be on the lookout for ways to develop your own skills: take extra courses, look for opportunities to speak, make presentations or appear on radio or television. Don't back away from difficult assignments. They will help you grow.

Here are some other factors to consider:

◆ **Risk.** Don't brush off the possibility of self-employment just because it scares you to death. Every successful entrepreneur felt exactly the same way. Kristie Strasen, a New York fabric designer, was terrified at the prospect when she left Tandem Mills, a Canadian textile firm, in 1986 to set up her own business. "I realized a long time ago that I'm not the sort of person that does better work with the dogs nipping at my heels," she says. But after more than a decade as a successful designer, she's not looking over her shoulder anymore to see if the wolf is at the door. Putting all your eggs in one basket is risky, too.

◆ **Marketing.** Many people with terrific skills simply don't know how to let people know that they're available. Think about how you will do this.

◆ **Fees.** You must be able to figure out how to set yours and stick to your guns. When Olimpia Meccia, a jewelry designer, left Tiffany & Company to set up her own business, she found that clients would expect a lower fee if the piece they wanted was simple. "They're still getting all the knowledge I have," she says. "Just because they choose not to use everything I know doesn't mean they don't have to pay for it."

◆ **Professional growth.** When you work for yourself, you will have no mentors. You must constantly weigh the relative merits of pumping out more work or, say, attending seminars to learn more about your specialty. You must also choose between projects that pay well but offer little challenge and those that pay less but offer opportunity for growth.

CALCULATE
RETIREMENT NEEDS

"Boring," I hear you saying. True. And sobering, too. But spend a moment anyway. Working longer will be a necessity for most Americans. But none of us will work forever. We must still save and prepare for the portion of our life when we do not work.

There are lots of charts, tables, and software programs to help you find out how much money you will need for retirement. Most assume that you will need about 75 to 80 percent of your working income to maintain a comfortable lifestyle in retirement.

Here is a chart that I like prepared by Steven E. Norwitz, vice president at T. Rowe Price & Associates, the Baltimore-based mutual fund company, because it gives you an idea of what you should have saved depending on how far you are from retirement. For younger people, those numbers seem easier to grapple with. Your savings goal is expressed as a multiple of your current income.

The chart *(at right)* also clearly illustrates how you can reach your goal by saving less if you choose a more aggressive investment strategy. Norwitz looked at three different investment strategies. The first is aggressive, with 80 percent invested in stocks and 20 percent in bonds before retirement and 65 percent in stocks, 35 percent in bonds after retirement.

The moderate strategy assumes a mix of 65 percent in stocks and 35 percent in bonds during working years and 50/50 after retirement. The conservative investor splits his money 50/50 between stocks and bonds during the working years and keeps just 35 percent in stocks during retirement.

YEARS TO RETIREMENT	INVESTMENT STRATEGY		
	AGGRESSIVE	MODERATE	CONSERVATIVE
0	957%	1046%	1048%
5	675%	773%	890%
10	463%	558%	676%
15	307%	393%	505%
20	193%	268%	369%
25	109%	172%	261%
30	48%	98%	174%
35	3%	42%	105%

To develop the numbers, Norwitz made the following assumptions:

◆ that you want to replace 75 percent of your pretax income at retirement and that that amount increases with the inflation rate every year;

◆ that you save 8 percent of your annual income between now and retirement in a pretax account and that your income grows at the rate of inflation;

◆ that you will spend 25 years in retirement and use all of the money you have saved at the end of that time period;

◆ that all distributions are pretax.

The chart certainly points to the value of starting early and putting money in stocks. It is also sobering. If you earn $75,000 and you are ready to retire, you need a nest egg of about $750,000. If you're there, great. If you're not, don't despair. Few Americans have managed to meet all their financial needs in neat little packages like this. Keep working on it. Start thinking, too, about the transition you will make to your retirement life. If you're far short of your goal, you'll probably need to work a little more and save a little longer.

REFINE YOUR PROJECTIONS

STEP

5

Calculating retirement needs is not fun. But figuring out what changes you can make might be—particularly if they are nearly effortless. A good retirement software program can help you look at all your assets—retirement accounts like 401(k)s, pension plans, and IRAs as well as the equity in your home, the cash value in your life insurance and other savings and assets you might have—and translate them into retirement income.

You can plug in your salary and your current rate of savings, and see how much you fall short. Then you can see what happens if you save a little more or if you invest a bit more aggressively. If you are in your twenties, the result of even a tiny change can be startling. But wherever you are, changing your habits just a bit can make a big difference.

The best place to begin is your company's human resources department. Most employers want their employees to grasp the enormity of the need to save for retirement. And they're doing what they can to help. Many of them provide tools that are customized to use your company's 401(k) plan and pension to help you see what you can expect from them and where you might fall short.

For example, the IBM Corp., a traditional leader in the employee benefits area, issued a piece of software to every employee in 1991 to help him or her chart a course to retirement by manipulating budget assumptions and pension options. IBM's purpose was two-fold. It wanted to help employees plan. But it also wanted to make certain they didn't stay around too long. At the time, IBM had built an enviable reputation for avoiding layoffs. And the company was still hoping to avoid them. (We all know that didn't work out.)

The software package showed employees what they could expect in inflation-adjusted dollars from each portion of the company's retirement plan as well as from Social Security. It also helped them determine how they could change the picture by saving, say, 1 percent more of salary or taking a little bit more investment risk to produce an additional 1 percentage point in return. It showed how much of a gap an employee faced between expected income and what might be needed at retirement. And it suggested ways to close the gap, such as contributing more to a 401(k) plan. The IBM story is an interesting one because it illustrates how what was once the mightiest of companies was forced to trim benefits to stay in the game—and how it tried to help employees as it did so.

In the years since IBM introduced its package, most major employers have developed something similar. Check to see if your employer has one. If not, consider one of the good—but inexpensive—products from one of the leading mutual fund companies. Fidelity Investments (800-544-8888), T. Rowe Price (800-638-5660), and the Vanguard Group (800-662-7447) each offer a quality software package for just $15. Of course, the programs feature the mutual funds from that particular fund group. But you don't have to buy them.

You might also check on the World Wide Web for retirement planning worksheets. The Mutual Fund Education Alliance, a trade group for funds that are sold directly over the phone or through the mail—like those listed above—provides retirement worksheets at its Web site (www.mfea.com), as well as links to the Web sites of other mutual fund companies.

It *is* sobering to see just how much money it will cost to support yourself without any employment income coming in. But don't get discouraged about it. Start saving. Learn about investing. And make plans for how you will supplement this nest egg.

CONSIDER WHAT YOU'RE LIKELY
TO GET FROM A PENSION

STEP

6

Some of today's retirees enjoy rich pension benefits from corporate plans, many of which were set up after World War II to attract workers and to keep them in a booming economy. These plans are called defined benefit plans because they define the annual pension benefit you receive. The employer foots the bill for the entire plan, putting the money aside, investing it, and taking the responsibility for making certain it is available to pay out benefits.

Defined benefit plans were designed to reward loyal employees who spent their entire careers with one company. The benefit is heavily weighted toward the later working years, when the employee's salary is highest. A good plan should replace about 50 percent of income for an employee with 30 years' service.

But few Americans at midcareer today have spent their career at a single employer. In recent years, workers over 25 have changed jobs every 5.7 years, on average, according to a retirement study done by the Investment Company Institute, the mutual fund industry trade group, based on figures from the Bureau of Labor Statistics. In fact, many 45-year-olds are not vested in any pension plan at all.

The benefit from a traditional pension is calculated as a percent of your final salary times years of service with the company. A typical defined benefit plan might provide 1.2 percent to 1.5 percent of the average of your final three years of compensation times your years of service as an annual pension. Suppose your average salary over your last three years of work is $100,000 a year. Then 1.5 percent is $1,500. If you have been with the company for 40 years, your annual pension would be $60,000. Work 25 years and you earn $37,500; five years earns you $7,500.

So job hopping reduces the benefit substantially. When you leave an employer at age 40, your pension benefit at age 65 will be calculated based on the salary you earned 25 years earlier, with no adjustment for inflation. For example, Dale R. Detlefs spent 18 years with "a large industrial company with an excellent pension plan," leaving when he was 47. When he retired in 1992 at age 65, his pension from this previous employer was "just enough to cover my utility bill," he says.

To illustrate the penalty for job hoppers, actuary Ethan E. Kra calculated benefits for three employees, each with 40 years of employment, the same final salary, and the same pension benefit formula. The first, who spent all 40 years with the same employer, receives 60 percent of his final salary as a pension benefit. The second, who worked at two employers for 20 years each, receives 39 percent of final salary. The third, who worked at four employers for 10 years each, receives just 31 percent.

Obviously, there are many more important things that will shape your career decisions than what type of pension you will receive. Still, it is important to understand how benefits in these plans are affected by the salary you earn and your years of service.

By working longer, you increase the time when you will have a regular income, increase your assets and eventual pension, and decrease the years spent consuming those assets. Federal law mandates that your employer must continue to credit years of service for pension purposes if you work beyond normal retirement age. If you receive salary increases, you will also be increasing your pay for purposes of calculating your pension. The eventual pension increase reflects what is called an "actuarial equivalent," meaning you should get the same amount of money over your expected lifespan no matter when you decide to retire.

DON'T BANK ON SOCIAL SECURITY

STEP

7

The Social Security system is in deep trouble. A 1997 article in *Financial Planning* magazine pointed out that many corporations are warning employees not to count on Social Security. Henry Montgomery, a Minneapolis-based financial planner, advises clients to start viewing Social Security as a subsidy for lower-income individuals rather than a benefit that we will all collect. "You may get something, but you probably won't get it until age 70, and it won't be worth what you think it will be worth," Montgomery says.

Social Security income has never been adequate to provide for a comfortable retirement. But for many of today's retirees, it provides a comfortable base. Even that is changing. And it will change rapidly as the baby boomers begin to retire around the year 2010. If the system were to continue as it is today, it is expected to start paying out more each year in benefits than it collects in taxes after 2012.

Changing demographics are straining the system. When the first Social Security checks were mailed out in 1937, more than 40 workers were paying withholding taxes to support each retiree. In 1950, it was 16 workers to one retiree. Today just three workers support each retiree. And that will drop to two workers per retiree by the year 2030.

Americans are living much longer, too. When the system was set up in the '30s, few people lived long enough to collect Social Security. Those who retire today may have 20 to 30 years ahead of them. That means that retirees are collecting much more than they paid into the system, putting more of a burden on working people.

Some patches have already been applied. For instance, normal retirement age will increase gradually to age 67—and then perhaps beyond. Higher-income retirees pay tax on benefits, another trend that is certain to accelerate. So it is clear that middle and upper income taxpayers at the beginning of the 21st century will get a haircut on their Social Security benefits.

But the government's largest and most popular program is unlikely to disappear. Neither political party is eager to accept the blame for cutting benefits and/or increasing taxes. That became clear when a presidential advisory panel, after debating the problem for two years, reported in early 1997 that action must be taken "as early as possible" to save the system. Everybody read the report and commented on it. But nobody wanted to administer the harsh medicine.

Still, it's worth looking at the conclusions drawn by this group because they sketch in broad outline possible changes to the system. The panel came up with three distinct solutions to bail out Social Security. The only area of agreement was that each group believed that some of the system's funds must be invested in the stock market to provide higher returns. (All the money is now invested in U.S. government bonds.)

The first group, supported by the panel's labor representatives, wants to maintain existing benefits by increasing payroll taxes by 1.6 percent and reducing benefits slightly in the future. The second group would provide for a tax increase that would go into private retirement accounts. It would also increase the retirement age and reduce benefits for middle- and upper-income recipients.

The third group would move toward "privatizing" Social Security by diverting a portion of the payroll tax into mandatory personal retirement accounts. This solution would preserve benefits for those 55 and older. It would also lift the retirement age, increase the taxes, and provide a floor benefit from the current system while depending more on the private retirement accounts.

CHECK YOUR SOCIAL SECURITY EARNINGS AND BENEFITS

STEP 8

Don't despair over Social Security. A 1996 study by the Employee Benefits Research Institute in Washington, D.C., found that 79 percent of workers did not believe Social Security will continue to provide the benefits it does today. And 23 percent did not expect to receive any benefits at all. But don't get bogged down in all the brouhaha over the shortfall in the system. You will get something from Social Security. It's just not clear yet what it will be. "The idea that Social Security is not going to be here is absolute foolishness," Minneapolis financial planner Henry Montgomery tells clients. "But when you look ahead 15 years, the benefits it will pay become imponderable."

Even if benefits do shrink before you retire—or especially if they shrink—you want to be certain that you get what you've earned from the system. To do that, it's important to check regularly on your earnings and expected benefits. You should make a note to do so every three years.

Social Security benefits are based on your lifetime earnings. If your earnings are reported inaccurately to Social Security or if the Social Security Administration records them inaccurately, it could affect your benefits. The Social Security Administration is not required to correct any error in an earnings statement that is more than three years old. That puts the burden on you to make certain your records are accurate and up to date. It is particularly important to check your earnings report if you change your name or if you marry and report your earnings on a joint return when you did not do so before. The Social Security Administration has also been known to lose earnings figures for women who marry and keep their maiden names.

To check your earnings and benefits, call Social Security at 800-772-1213 and follow the automated instructions to request a copy of form SSA-7004. It should arrive within two or three weeks. When you receive the form, fill it out and send it back in.

Within a month, you should receive your report. On the first page, you will see a message from the Commissioner of Social Security. The message being mailed out in 1997 assures us that "the Social Security Board of Trustees projects that the system has enough money to pay full benefits for the next 32 years. This means there is time for the Congress to make changes to safeguard the program's financial future."

At the bottom of the page are the facts you provided on the form, including name, Social Security number, date of birth, recent earnings, and the age you plan to stop working. On the second page is a report of your earnings and estimated taxes paid. Check to make certain that you were credited for all your earnings. You are required to pay tax up to the Social Security wage base, which is $65,400 for 1997. So if you earn $100,000, your earnings will be recorded as $65,400. However, there is no limit on earnings taxed for Medicare, so you should see your full earnings reported for each year since 1992 under the Medicare column.

On the next page you will see estimated monthly benefits if you retire at age 62, at full-retirement age— which might be 65, 66, or 67, depending on when you were born—and at age 70. The benefits at age 70 reflect credits for working longer. There are also some details about disability benefits. If there is a mistake in your record, call 800-537-7005 to request a correction. Then go through the process again in one year to make certain it has been corrected.

TAKE A LOOK AT TAXES

STEP

9

No matter what your age, your income, or your goals, taxes will figure somehow in your investment choices. What you pay in taxes has a great deal to do with how much money is left for you to spend. Obviously, the less tax you pay, the more you have.

Unfortunately for those who would like to do some tax planning, the Tax Reform Act of 1986 made sweeping changes in the way Americans pay taxes, eliminating most tax shelters and writeoffs in exchange for lower rates. Starting in 1987, top individual rates were reduced from myriad rates ranging up to 70 percent to just two: 15 percent and 28 percent. Since then, of course, rates have been creeping up again, so that the top rate in 1997 is 39.6 percent. But the difference today is that there are few tax shelters available to shield money from that stiff tax rate.

The Taxpayer Relief Act of 1997 provided a bit of help with the new Roth IRA, the college IRA, breaks on capital gains taxes, and tax-free gains for many homeowners who sell and make a profit. Still, one of the best of the tax shelters that we have today is the 401(k) plan. Tax Reform '86 had something to say about 401(k) plans, too. It reduced the maximum an individual could contribute in a single year from $30,000 to $7,000, a number that is indexed with inflation and that rose to $10,000 for 1998. It also imposed a stiff penalty of 10 percent on money that is withdrawn from 401(k) plans before age 59½.

But even with those changes, a 401(k) plan is a powerhouse—so much so that you should probe into a plan's provisions when you are job hunting. It will not be the deciding factor in a career move. But it could be a tie breaker.

A word here about tax definitions:

◆ **Tax advantaged** is a catchall term that can be used to describe practically any kind of investment. It means nothing specific.

◆ **Tax deferred** means that current taxes are not due on an investment. The money in annuities and cash value life insurance policies enjoys tax deferral on investment earnings. Taxes are not due until the money is withdrawn.

◆ **Tax free** means that no taxes are due ever on an investment. That is the case for some types of bonds issued by federal and state governments. Municipal bonds, which are issued by state, city, or other local governments to pay for projects, are free of federal taxes. Sometimes called "munis," many are also free of state and local taxes.

◆ **Pretax** means that you may use money for some purpose before you pay tax on it. Sometimes you never pay tax on it. That's the case with money you are permitted to spend for certain health care or dependent care needs.

When you contribute to a 401(k) plan, you use pretax dollars. The money is subtracted from the compensation on which you pay tax that year. So if you earn $65,000 and you put $5,000 into a 401(k) plan, your income will be reported as $60,000. Every state except Pennsylvania also permits you to subtract the 401(k) contribution from your compensation for state tax purposes.

Suppose your combined federal and state tax bracket is 35 percent. If you took your $5,000 as taxable income, you would pay $1,750 in federal and state taxes and receive just $3,250 to spend. When you contribute to the 401(k) plan, you're getting the full $5,000 in your account. Your 401(k) plan also gives you continued tax deferral—or postponement of taxes—on both the money you contribute and the investment earnings on that money until you withdraw your money from the plan.

CONSIDER THE POWER
OF COMPOUNDING

STEP

10

Investors are forever looking for that one magic investment that will make their fortune. The closest thing you will get to magic in investing is the compounding of interest. What that means is that your earnings generate their own earnings so that, seemingly by magic, money begets more money and the money you invested doubles, triples, and quadruples. Albert Einstein called the compounding of interest the greatest mathematical discovery of all time.

When an inexperienced investor thinks about saving for a goal, he typically estimates how much he needs and divides it by the number of years—or months—he has to meet his goal. So to save $10,000 in five years, he would need to stash away $2,000 a year.

But time is the magic ingredient here. The power of compounding means that even a tiny sum of money can grow into a colossus given enough time. *The Price Waterhouse Personal Financial Advisor* (Times Mirror, 1995; $15) provides a couple of interesting examples. Consider the $24 paid by the Dutch for the island of Manhattan in 1626. Had it been invested at 7 percent, it would have grown to more than $1.9 trillion by the end of 1997.

Of course, as Price Waterhouse points out, few of us have three or four centuries to wait for our money to grow. But some of us *are* young. And for the young, time is a wonderful asset. Let's assume a 21-year-old wants to accumulate $1 million to retire at age 65. Assuming that the money returns an average of 10.2 percent a year, which is the average return for common stocks since 1926, this young worker would need to put away just $1,185 a year. (The example assumes that you are investing in a tax-deferred account like a 401(k) plan.) If our young worker could invest a bit more—$2,200 a year—he could stop investing after 10 years and still reach his goal. His $22,000 investment would grow to $1 million by age 65.

Of course, some of us are *not* young. But time—and the rate of return—make an enormous difference for every investor. Even if you are already 65, you might have 20 or 30 years ahead of you—plenty of time to take advantage of the power of compounding.

Notice how the examples in the Price Waterhouse guide assume that the young investor got a 10.2 percent return on his money—the average return of the stock market over the past 70 years. Had you stashed your money in a bank account at 3 or 4 percent, you would not have reached your goal.

So investment return is a function of both time and return. To see how the interplay between these two works, investors use a handy rule of thumb called "The Rule of 72." If you pick an annual rate of return and divide it into 72, the answer will show you how long it will take your money to double if you earn that return. Try it. If you earn 3 percent on a bank savings account, your money will double in 24 years. But if you are an active and aggressive investor who can figure out a way to earn 20 percent, your money will double in 3.6 years. (Few investors do that well over time.) At a 10 percent return, it would double in 7.2 years.

As you set up your 401(k) and choose your investments, keep in mind the power of time and the magic of compounding. Even a small amount of money that earns a low rate of return can grow into a mountain. But if you can invest a substantial amount of money and earn a good return, it can help you achieve independence.

Although it is not implicit in compounding of interest, this principle works best with money left untouched. Trading, buying, selling, and fussing with your money all diminish the return.

START EARLY

STEP

11

If you're 25 years old, saving sounds like punishment. You've probably just finished four to six years of college and money was tight. And now you're ready to spend. In most cases, there's not enough money from that first job to stretch to buy all the things you need.

But consider this: You may not have lots of money. But you have something far more valuable: Time. Time can turn a grain of sand into a mountain or $1,000 into a million bucks, thanks to the power of compound interest. Compounding means your money can earn money. If a 25-year-old puts $10,000 in an investment that earns 8 percent a year and leaves it for 40 years, he will have more than $200,000, thanks to the magic of compounding. Of course, few 25-year-olds have $10,000 to spare. But putting money away regularly is the best way to put yourself on the road to riches.

Parents and teachers have tried to teach this simple lesson to children and students for countless years. Most young adults have ignored the lesson and— instead of saving—run up big debts to buy all those things they've wanted, but couldn't afford in their parents' homes or in college.

Think of it this way: The decisions you make about money have little to do with economics, dollars and cents, how much you have or how much you earn. Instead, they have to do with psychology: with how you feel about yourself and your habits.

The research of Tahira K. Hira, a professor of personal finance and consumer behavior at Iowa State University in Ames, confirms that. Hira spent several years studying personal bankruptcies in Scotland, Japan, and the United States, looking for patterns among those who ran into financial difficulties. She found them: low self-esteem, difficult family relationships, unhappy experiences at school. But she also

IF YOU START AT AGE 25 and put away just $25 a month until age 65, here is how much you will have depending on how much your money earns:

4 percent	$29,648
6 percent	$50,036
8 percent	$87,857
10 percent	$159,420

If you can put away $50 a month:

4 percent	$ 59,295
6 percent	$100,072
8 percent	$175,714
10 percent	$318,839

If you can up it to $75, here's what you'll have in 40 years:

4 percent	$ 88,943
6 percent	$150,109
8 percent	$263,571
10 percent	$478,259

And if you could put away $100 each month and earn 10 percent, you will be on your way to becoming a millionaire:

4 percent	$118,590
6 percent	$200,145
8 percent	$351,428
10 percent	$637,678

found that many people with money problems could address them by facing up to them.

If you can establish a habit of regular saving when you are just starting out in your career, it will be one of the most important things you ever do for yourself. Make it small to start. Just $10 a week if you like. But make the decision to get started. And discipline yourself to do it regularly.

COMPARE A 401(K) TO AN IRA

STEP 12 Both 401(k) plans and IRAs are tax-deferred retirement savings plans. Money contributed to either one grows, without a bite for taxes, until you retire. But there are some important differences in the two kinds of plans. If you must make a choice between the two, you should understand them.

You can contribute to both. But if you contribute to a 401(k), a contribution of up to $2,000 that you make to an IRA will be tax deductible only if you are:

a. single and earn less than $30,000

b. married filing jointly and earn less than $50,000 together with your spouse.

You may get a partial deduction if you are:

a. single and earn between $30,000 and $40,000

b. married filing jointly and earn between $50,000 and $60,000 as a household. These limits will increase to between $50,000 and $60,000 for single filers by 2005, and between $80,000 and $100,000 for married filing jointly by 2007.

If you earn more than these amounts, you can still make a nondeductible contribution to your IRA. But that is clearly less advantageous than contributing to a 401(k) plan. You may also elect not to participate in your 401(k) plan and decide instead to fund a deductible IRA. Eligibility is phased out for households earning between $150,000 and $160,000 if one spouse is a participant in a pension plan. If you earn more, you can still make a contribution to a Roth IRA *(see* **STEP 13***)* or a nondeductible IRA.

How should you decide between a 401(k) and an IRA? The 401(k) is more attractive in almost every case. The most obvious reason is that most plans provide an employer match. If yours does, the 401(k) plan is clearly the best choice. A 401(k) plan also allows you to contribute more—$9,500 for 1997—

than the $2,000 you can put in an IRA.

So even if your employer does not provide a match, there are reasons to go with the 401(k) provided it has good investment options. Saving is practically painless: Regular deductions are made from each paycheck, eliminating the trouble of deciding whether or not to invest. That helps you take advantage of dollar cost averaging *(see **STEP 52**)*, a superior method of investing that allows you to buy more shares of your mutual fund when the market is down, less when it is up.

Finally, a 401(k) is what the government refers to as a tax-qualified plan. When Congress makes pension rules, they are often different for qualified plans than for other types of retirement plans. For example, 10-year forward averaging of lump sum withdrawals is available only on money that is taken from qualified plans. This is a favorable tax treatment that permits you to treat a lump sum as if you received it over 10 years, which considerably lowers the tax bill. (Ten-year averaging is being phased out and is available only to those who were born before January 1, 1936.) Also, in 1996, Congress passed a law saying that those who continue to work beyond age 70½ need not begin mandatory withdrawals from their retirement accounts. But it applied only to qualified plans, not IRAs. The money in a qualified plan can usually be rolled into a similar plan at another employer. And the assets in a qualified plan are protected in bankruptcy. In many states, IRA assets do not have that protection.

There are different rules for getting the money out, too. Withdrawing money from either plan before age 59½ usually means that you must pay a 10 percent penalty. So with an IRA, you *can* get the money out if you are willing to pay the penalty. But you cannot withdraw money from a 401(k) plan unless you qualify for very stringent hardship withdrawal rules. On the other hand, most 401(k) plans permit loans for almost any reason. You can never borrow from your IRA.

TAKE A LOOK AT
THE NEW ROTH IRA

STEP 13 If you're baffled by the provisions of the Taxpayer Relief Act of 1997, you're not alone. Experts say this is one of the most complex tax bills ever passed. One provision you should be concerned with as you're looking at retirement savings options, though, is the Roth IRA, named for Senator William Roth of Delaware, a long-time campaigner for retirement accounts. This new IRA permits taxpayers within certain income limits to contribute up to $2,000 a year to a new type of retirement account. The contribution is not tax deductible. But there some big advantages:

1 Withdrawals from the account are completely tax free. Taxpayers who can leave the money untouched for a long period of time will almost always do better with this open-ended savings vehicle, thanks to the power of compounding.

2 There is no mandatory withdrawal schedule. You need never take the money out during your lifetime. It can continue to grow tax-deferred. "If you live to 80 or 90, you don't have to take anything out, and you can keep contributing," says Gregory Kolojeski, a tax attorney who is developing software to compare the Roth IRA to the deductible IRA.

3 There is no 10 percent penalty made on early withdrawals before age 59$\frac{1}{2}$ provided you withdraw the contributions you made, not the earnings. That means your money is not out of reach until retirement.

4 You can continue to contribute to the account as long as you continue to earn employment income. With the traditional IRA, you cannot after age 70$\frac{1}{2}$.

5 The money is not included in taxable income when you withdraw it. That can be important, for example, for those who receive Social Security income. Money from a traditional IRA *is* included in taxable income, which can make Social Security benefits taxable for some people.

"When you have distributions from a regular IRA, it is taxable income, which pulls your income up," says Robert S. Keebler, a financial planner in Green Bay, Wisconsin. "So $1 in IRA income might increase your taxable income by $1.85 because it pulls your Social Security benefits into the equation." But that's not the case with distribtuions from a Roth IRA.

The tax bill left intact the traditional, deductible IRA, with a couple of improvements, and the old, nondeductible IRA. The income limits to contribute to the deductible IRA will be increased gradually to $50,000 to $60,000 in 2005 for single filers and $80,000 to $100,000 in 2007 for joint filers, giving many more people the opportunity to use these plans. For 1998, the limits are $30,000 for the full contribution for singles, which is gradually phased out until it disappears at $40,000. For couples filing jointly the 1998 limit is $50,000 for a full contribution, phased out until it disappears at $60,000.

The maximum contribution that can be made to a Roth IRA is phased out for single filers with adjusted gross income between $95,000 and $110,000 and for couples filing jointly with adjusted gross income between $150,000 and $160,000.

Contributions may be split between the three plans. But no taxpayer is permitted to make more than $2,000 in total IRA contributions per year. Most experts who have examined the Roth IRA say that it is a better deal for nearly every taxpayer who has a choice between a traditional, tax-deductible IRA and the new Roth. "The Roth IRA is almost always better," says Steven Norwitz, a vice president at T. Rowe Price Associates in Baltimore, who has run models comparing the various types of retirement accounts.

CONTRIBUTE, CONTRIBUTE

STEP
14

Navigating the employment landscape today is tough. It requires plenty of ingenuity to figure out how to make a living, hone your skills, build your résumé, and juggle your financial needs. Your 401(k) plan can become a powerful tool to help you create financial independence.

Too many people fail to use it. Eligible 401(k) investors are walking away from an estimated $6 billion a year in free 401(k) money, according to a study done by Access Research Inc., the Windsor, Connecticut, research firm. Nearly 12 million eligible American workers either fail to participate in their company's 401(k) plan or don't invest enough to take full advantage of free matching contributions from their employers, which are typically 50 cents on every $1 contributed up to a certain maximum portion of salary.

It is younger employees and those at lower salary levels who are least likely to contribute. Yet these are the employees who can profit most from a 401(k) plan. In fact, the 401(k) plan is even a better bet than a traditional pension for a younger worker. "There's a heavy tilt in favor of younger people in these plans," says Judith Whinfrey, senior manager at Hewitt Associates, benefits consultants in Lincolnshire, Illinois. "The contribution is the same no matter what the age, but you have all those years for the dollars to compound."

The 401(k) plan is great for job hoppers, too because the plans are portable. When you leave your job, the money is yours. You can roll it into an IRA, leave it with your employer—in an account in your name, of course—or move it to your new employer's 401(k) plan. You can even use it to tide you through a rough spot if you are desperate. Although it's not advisable to spend your retirement nest egg, knowing you have one might help you sleep better.

If the 401(k) is better for young workers and for job hoppers, who benefits from the traditional pension? Older workers. We asked Whinfrey how an employee might get the optimal pension benefit, provided he could make whatever career moves he liked. She calculated that the way to get the maximum benefits would be to spend the first half of your career at a company—or companies with a defined contribution plan like a 401(k), tuck the money away faithfully, and then move to a company with a rich defined benefit plan 15 years before retirement. "It's the absolute perfect way to play your career," Whinfrey said.

She compared the pension benefits of four employees, each with a final salary of $150,000. The first executive, who spent his 30-year career at a company with a traditional defined benefit pension, retired with an annual benefit of $67,500. But the executive who spent his first 15 years at a company with a 401(k) plan and the second 15 years with a defined benefit plan retired with a pension of $74,110. A worker who spent his entire career with a 401(k) and a worker who started with a defined benefit plan and switched to a 401(k) at midpoint did worse.

What's at work here is the power of compounding on money tucked away in the early years combined with a benefit based on the fatter salary of the later years.

The message is a simple one: Contribute whatever you can to a 401(k) plan as early as possible, even if you start with just a few dollars a month. If your employer provides *any* type of match, contribute up to the limit to capture it. This is one of the most important things you can do to establish your financial independence.

BUY DISABILITY INSURANCE

STEP 15 What does disability insurance have to do with a book on 401(k)s? A lot. Your income—and your ability to keep bringing it in and enhancing it—is your single biggest asset. It stands to reason, then, that the biggest threat to you is an illness or accident that would cut off that income. If you are over age 21, there is one chance in three that you will be disabled before you retire, according to the Health Insurance Association of America, an industry trade group.

You need health insurance to pay the bills. And you need disability income insurance to keep your income intact. Many employees assume that they have adequate coverage through their employee benefits plan and that they don't need to buy their own policy. But 75 to 80 percent of American companies do not have disability policies, according to Jane Ann Schiltz, director of individual disability marketing at Northwestern Mutual in Milwaukee. Even if your company offers a disability plan, there are a couple of good reasons to buy your own.

If you buy your own policy and pay the premiums, benefits are tax free. If your employer pays the premiums, benefits are taxable. In order to buy disability insurance, you need good health and an income. If you wait until you need it, you may not qualify.

What should you look for when you buy a policy? Disability policies are extremely complex and expensive. The more complex, the more expensive. "There are a lot of bells and whistles on disability policies that significantly increase the premium amount," says Michael J. Chasnoff, a financial planner in Cincinnati. "Too often people buy features that they are unaware of that add a lot to the premium."

For instance, an automatic cost-of-living adjustment can add 50 percent to the premium. A policy that pays benefits for life rather than to age 65 can add 75 percent to the premium. Both are valuable features, to be sure. But for most of us they are not affordable. Focus instead on getting the highest possible monthly benefit. "Get high basic coverage and leave out some of the extras," says Glenn S. Daily, an insurance consultant in New York and author of *The Individual Investor's Guide to Low-Load Insurance Products.*

Another popular feature in a disability policy is coverage that will pay a benefit if you cannot work in your own occupation. But Daily argues that if you could make the same amount of money doing something else, you do not really need additional income from your disability policy. Daily suggests you spend your disability premium for high basic coverage and coverage for residual disability, which means that you will get a partial benefit if you are partly disabled.

When you shop for a policy, check:

◆ **Waiting period.** This is comparable to a deductible on a medical plan. The longer you wait before drawing benefits, the lower the premium. Most planners recommend a 90-day waiting period. That means you would start collecting benefits four months after you are disabled—the 90-day wait and another 30 days before the insurer writes the check.

◆ **Benefit period.** You can buy a policy that will pay benefits for one, two, or five years, until you reach age 65 or for your lifetime. Planners recommend age 65. Lifetime coverage is extremely expensive.

◆ **Income replacement.** Look for a benefit that would replace 60 to 70 percent of your total compensation. If you earn $100,000 a year, your policy should pay $60,000.

Before you buy a policy, check the income replacement policy at USAA Life in San Antonio, Texas. This company, which got its start in 1922 providing insurance only to military officers, sells quality products at competitive prices over the phone (800-531-8000).

PART

2

401(k) Plans
THE BASICS

VER THE PAST decade tens of thousands of American workers have been shoved aside. What a waste of talent! Equally disheartening are those who have lost their gumption instead of their jobs; those who have let the sweeping changes in corporate America blur their focus and waste their spirit.

In the fall of 1996, I wrote an article for *Modern Maturity* magazine about a rash of lawsuits that were brought by employers against current or former employers, largely as a result of changing corporate values. They had to do with such things as age discrimination, misrepresentation of company benefits, and so forth. For example, one company shifted a group of workers into a new division of the company, and then told them that that division did not have health insurance. Another man, who was contemplating early retirement, went to the human resources department to see if any sweetened retirement packages were in the works. Nope, the company officials said. So he retired. The following week, a buyout offer was announced that would have put several thousand dollars in his pocket.

Shortly after the article appeared, I received a letter from a man in Georgia who wrote to complain of the way his wife's employer had mistreated her. She had worked for many years in a corporate position for a large company. When she heard rumors that the company was planning to cut back its work force, she found another job—with a six-figure income. Shortly after she started her new job, her former employer did indeed downsize, offering generous severance packages to those in her former department. This man reasoned that his wife was cheated out of this money. The couple contacted both the employer and a lawyer but were unable to get a severance package for the wife. When he saw my story, he wrote to me asking for my help—three times.

This is a great example of someone who is heading off in the wrong direction. Don't fall victim to that. The workplace has become treacherous. You need all your wits—and your energy—to do a good job and set a course for yourself. The new employment contract *is* a short-term, temporary one. In recognition of that, many employers are beginning to provide skills training that will help employees move on when they are no longer needed by their employer. "This is the most exciting thing that's happening in employee benefits," says Richard Wald, a principal in the Minneapolis office of William M. Mercer Inc., benefits consultants. But you must be on your toes to learn about these programs. The notice might amount to nothing more than a note on the bulletin board or an item in the company newsletter, announcing courses on presentation skills or computer skills. Find out about them and sign up. Employers are also often eager to woo back former employees when the work load changes, Hal Lancaster wrote in his really fine column, "Managing Your Career," which runs in *The Wall Street Journal* on Tuesday. So keep your options open.

The workplace today offers you the perfect opportunity to take the optimist/pessimist test. Is the glass of life half empty or half full? Is your 401(k) plan a burden or an opportunity? What about your job? Your career? If you've been following along in this book up to this point, you've already discovered that 401(k) plans were not devised as a bonanza for employees. That doesn't mean you can't get a lot out of them. But you may as well understand that you're not the only one with something at stake. I think it will help you to squeeze the most out of your plan if you understand who's involved and what these players hope to accomplish.

LOOK AT THE PLAYERS

STEP

16

So often, the financial mistakes we make come from a lack of perspective. We view the landscape from ground level in the forest. To make sound financial decisions, you should understand who you're dealing with and what vested interests your partners have.

The three players involved in a 401(k) plan are your employer, who sponsors the plan; you and the other employees who participate in the plan—or don't participate, as the case may be; and the government, which regulates the plan, aiming to make certain that employees are treated fairly, that the company doesn't take off with the money, and that the Internal Revenue Service eventually gets its money from the plan in the form of taxes.

Each of the three makes demands on the 401(k) and each gets something out of it. Of course, you should be concerned about what you get out of the plan. But that will depend a lot on you and your understanding of the process. Over the years that I've been writing about personal finance, I've received hundreds of letters from readers who made big financial mistakes simply because they misunderstood these rules and mistakenly believed that the entire process was set up to benefit *them*.

When the first 401(k) plan was set up in 1981, it was designed almost *entirely* to appeal to employers who had a problem attracting lower-paid workers to a retirement plan. If lower-paid workers don't contribute, the government nixes the plan as a perk only for the higher paid. So the carrot for lower paids was the company match.

Under the traditional defined benefit pension plans, which were the norm at the time, employers were responsible for setting all of the money aside for pensions, for investing it and for paying it out. It didn't take employers long to see that providing a company match in a 401(k) plan would be much cheaper than funding the whole pension.

Critics are quick to say that employers have abdicated their responsibility to employees by doing this. "The movement to 401(k) plans is a catastrophe for workers and dangerous for employers," John Langbein, law professor at Yale Law School, told a group of financial advisers in Palm Beach, Florida, in 1997. Langbein's criticism stems from his belief that employees don't know how to invest. "Bucky Six-Pack simply doesn't know how to make investment choices," Langbein said.

But pointing the finger will not solve your retirement problems. The growth of 401(k) plans coincided with a revolution in American business. Bloated companies were looking for ways to trim down, shift costs, and improve their bottom lines. The 401(k) plan was one good way to do it. Thanks to reduced employee benefit costs, American companies have become competitive in the global economy again. But they have also broken the old rules of the employment contract. They no longer promise to take care of their employees, either today or tomorrow. Not surprisingly, then, there has been a massive decline in employee loyalty over the past 15 years.

Arguing about whether it is right or wrong for your company to take care of you now and in retirement will not do you much good. You may as well be pragmatic about it and make the best use you can of the new employment contract, tenuous as it is. The contract between workers and employers *has* changed dramatically. This is a time of fewer promotions, lower salary increases, just-in-time inventory, more work force reductions—and increased employee responsibility for retirement. You will be much better off in your work—and in your life—if you try to use this to your advantage.

CONSIDER YOUR
EMPLOYER'S AGENDA

STEP

17

Most employers who use 401(k) plans want to offer a good plan. They realize that employees have more responsibility for their own financial needs today and they want them to succeed. On the other hand, they do not want to be on the hook if the employees fail to save enough.

So employers attempt to achieve a delicate balance. They know that novice investors put too little into the stock market and too much into guaranteed investments, like GICs or guaranteed investment contracts. But they are afraid to advise employees to move to stocks to improve their returns for fear the employees may lose money and blame them—or, worse yet, sue them.

Of course, the government gets involved here, too, and mandates that the employer do certain things. There are two basic types of 401(k) plans. In one, the employer has fiduciary responsibility for acting in the best interest of employees. It can offer whatever investment options it wants, including only company stock. But the employer who chooses this plan faces liability if employees lose money because of bad investment decisions.

The other type of 401(k) plan relieves the employer of fiduciary responsibility provided it complies with certain rules. Those rules, which are referred to as 404 (c) regulations, effective on January 1, 1994, spell out just what it is that an employer must do if it wants limited protection from liability.

Employers who choose to comply with these regulations must offer at least three diversified investment choices that enable employees to construct portfolios with a wide variety of risk/return characteristics. Employer stock can be offered. But because it is not a diversified investment, it does not qualify as one of the three choices.

Under these regulations, employers must allow employees to shift between investment options at least once every three months. They must provide adequate disclosure of the options and some type of employee communication and education. Employers who comply will not be liable in the event of losses from bad investment decisions. But they will still be on the hook for a broad range of things like picking investment managers and making certain the options offered are good ones.

There is still a huge range of possibilities within these guidelines. Consider how two companies interpreted their 401(k) responsibilities. When Morningstar Inc., the Chicago company that made its reputation by rating mutual funds, set up a 401(k) plan in 1991, it selected a plan with one top-notch fund in each asset class, such as a U.S. large-company fund, a U.S. small-company fund, a bond fund, a money market fund, an international stock fund, and a natural resource fund for those employees who wanted a hedge. Setting up a portfolio with these funds is a simple matter for employees because each fund is a good one and is distinct from the others.

Let's look at what General Motors did. In 1995, G.M. had the largest 401(k) in the country with $12 billion in assets but just a handful of sleepy options. The automaker knew it needed more options but was apparently unwilling to go the route of Morningstar and put an implicit stamp of approval on a handful of funds.

So G.M. offered a complex plan with 37 choices. Predictably, many employees felt overwhelmed. "The G.M. plan just got better, but it also got a lot more complex and I don't have the time to do it on my own," said David Christeller, a G.M. engineer. Like hundreds of other employees, Christeller hired a broker to manage his 401(k) account for a fee.

CONSIDER THE
GOVERNMENT'S AGENDA

STEP 18 Why does the government always get involved in these stories? For a couple of reasons. First, the government loses billions a year in tax revenues because of the dollars that go into 401(k) plans. Perhaps you remember that tax reformers severely limited the availability of individual retirement accounts by writing the Tax Reform Act of 1986. That move was made to raise tax revenues by closing what some lawmakers viewed as a "loophole" that allowed taxpayers to funnel money into IRAs before they paid tax on it.

Some consultants, like Ted Benna, who developed the first 401(k) plan in 1981, worry that the same fate will befall 401(k) plans. As Congress casts about looking for more tax revenue, nothing is sacred. So Congress always has its eye on any money that has tax advantages—or where tax revenue is lost. And the Internal Revenue Service keeps a close eye on how the plans are set up and maintained to make certain no additional taxes are lost. For the same reason, Congress sets rules on when and how the money is withdrawn from these plans so that the government will eventually collect these lost tax dollars.

The Department of Labor is another player in the 401(k) plans. The labor department gets involved because 401(k) plans permit employers to provide part of employee compensation in the form of benefits rather than straight salary dollars in a paycheck. The DOL wants to be certain that the money employees receive as benefits is protected in these plans.

Like traditional pension plans, 401(k) plans are "qualified plans," which simply means that they qualify for preferential tax treatment. In the case of 401(k) plans, that tax treatment is all of the things we've been talking about: Participants are permitted to contribute money before they pay tax on it. And employers, too, are permitted to make matching pre-tax contributions.

Qualified plans must dot all the i's and cross all the t's if they are to maintain this special tax status. So 401(k) plans at private companies must follow strict rules outlined in the tax code and the Employee Retirement Income Security Act of 1974, or ERISA. These rules govern participation, vesting schedules, and nondiscrimination testing, among other elements, and they are enforced by the Department of Labor and the IRS and the Treasury Department.

In addition to making certain that it gets its tax dollars, the government wants to be certain that those tax dollars it gives up—at least temporarily—are used to benefit a broad range of employees, not just those highly paid executives who are setting up the plan. That's where the participation, vesting schedules, and nondiscrimination rules come in.

The government puts teeth in its regulations, too. A 401(k) plan that does not comply with all the rules can lose its special tax-qualified status or be "disqualified," a word that strikes fear in the hearts of employers and the benefits consultants who design these plans. If a plan is disqualified, the sponsor, or employer who sponsors the plan, loses the tax deduction for all the contributions it has made. The employer must pay back taxes and penalties on the unpaid tax.

Disqualification is bad news for participants, too. It means that they owe taxes on all the money they have contributed to the plan. Tax lawyers and consultants call this "the big stick," referring to the punishment for employers who fail to comply. "It's a lot of bang for the buck," says Rhonda Davis, a consultant in the Boston office of Hewitt Associates, benefits consultants. And that threat makes employers very eager to adhere to the rules laid down for qualified plans.

TURN THIS TO YOUR ADVANTAGE

STEP

19

A 401(k) plan is not as good as an inheritance. But, contrary to what a lot of critics say, it can be better than a traditional defined benefit pension where your employer foots the bill. A defined benefit plan sounds promising. But unless you spend your working career at one company, the results are likely to be disappointing.

And defined benefit plans enslave workers. For every worker who retires fulfilled from a happy career, there are probably a dozen who feel forced to stick with their employer—no matter how frustrated and bored they feel—because they need their pension. That hit home to me when I was heading into New York City on an Amtrak train in April 1997 after a freak spring snowstorm had caused five-hour delays. Once the passengers realized that they would never make it to their meetings and all the food and drinks in the snack car had been consumed, tension gave way to a sort of camaraderie and people began spilling their life stories.

The man in the seat behind me confided to his seatmate that he had taken early retirement at age 60 after 31 years as an engineer with the same company. He didn't have enough income to retire and knew he had to find work. Yet, "it was almost a relief to be forced to make a change," he said. "I was so bored there for all those years." Although he got good assignments and tackled each new one with enthusiasm, they might result in six months of interesting work followed by three or four or five years of complete boredom.

It occurred to me that this was the "lucky" employee that we've all been reading about—the worker of yesteryear who had lifetime employment. In fact, this man said, he had counseled his two daughters, who were in their thirties, to plan a career of job hopping, adding to their skills both by formal education and by working at different companies.

A 401(k) is the perfect tool for a job hopper. It buys you freedom. And you can turn the plan to your advantage. Your employer wants you to participate. If you are a lower-paid worker—today that means anything under $80,000—your employer *really* wants you to participate. That's because if workers under this income level don't participate, the higher paid can't contribute so much.

Think about the government's agenda for a moment. The government wants to make certain that 401(k) plans are not designed as a plum for the top executives. One of the ways it does that is to set up tests to make certain the plans do not discriminate in favor of the highly paid and against the rank and file.

To prove that it is nondiscriminatory it must meet certain tests. First it must be available to a broad group of employees. It may exclude, for example, union employees covered under a collective bargaining agreement if retirement benefits were a part of the agreement. It may also exclude employees who do not meet minimum eligibility requirements of age and length of service, nonresident aliens, and, of course, those who are terminated.

But plans must undergo broad tests to make certain they don't benefit only key employees. To perform this test, which is called the "actual deferral percentage test," employees are split into two groups, those who earn under $80,000 and those who earn over $80,000. Those in the higher income group can contribute, on average, just 2 percent more than the average contributed by the lower-income group.

So employers want "lower-paid" workers to contribute as much as possible, up to the legal limit of $9,500 for 1997. The more this group contributes as a percent of pay, the more the better-paid people can contribute.

LOOK AT THE
CONTRIBUTION LIMITS

STEP
20

Prior to the 1986 Tax Reform Act, participants were permitted to put a great deal of money into their 401(k) plans—up to $30,000 per year. But that tax reform law, which limited or eliminated many types of tax shelters, reduced, too, the amount that individuals could contribute to their 401(k) plans—to $7,000 in 1987, an amount that increases with inflation. The cap is tied to the consumer price index. Then a 1994 law decreed that the limit would rise only in $500 increments. So when inflation is low, the limit may remain the same for two years. Here are the deferral limits per year since 1986 Tax Reform:

1987	$7,000
1988	$7,313
1989	$7,627
1990	$7,979
1991	$8,475
1992	$8,728
1993	$8,994
1994	$9,240
1995	$9,240
1996	$9,500
1997	$9,500
1998	$10,000

For many employees, a more important limitation is the one imposed by the ADP, or actual deferral percentage, test. This test, which is typically called a "nondiscrimination test," is mandated by the government to determine that the plan is not unfairly favoring its higher-paid workers—defined under the 1996 tax act as those who earn more than $80,000 a year. To comply with government rules, every 401(k) plan must pass the test for each plan year.

Here's how the test works: Contributions made by employees earning less than $80,000 for 1997—the number is indexed—are tossed into a pool to determine the average percentage of salaries they contribute to the 401(k). These are the non-highly compensated employees—or non-HCEs in regulatory jargon. Then the average salary contribution is calculated for people who earn more than $80,000. The spread between the two groups is regulated: In most cases, it is limited to 2 percentage points. If the lower-paid group contributes 4 percent of salary on average, the higher-paid group can contribute no more than 6 percent on average.

Suppose a company discovers that its highly paid group is contributing an average of 7 percent and its lower-paid group only 4 percent. It must then return some money—which is taxable income—to the higher-paid group. A 1997 tax change says that the company must return the money first to those in this group who contributed the most actual dollars. So it is unlikely that participants in the highly compensated group would be permitted to contribute the full $10,000. However, the employer would be delighted if an employee earning $79,995 contributed the full $10,000—or 13 percent of his salary—because that would boost the average for the non-highly compensated group.

The salary deferral limit is only one of the stipulations you face when putting money into your 401(k) plan, though. Section 415 of the Internal Revenue Code imposes a limit on the total contribution made by and for an employee to a 401(k) plan. This includes the deferral limits just discussed as well as employee after-tax contributions, the employer match, and any other employer contributions such as profit-sharing contributions. The combination of all these contributions may not exceed the lesser of 25 percent of the participant's compensation or $30,000.

PAY ATTENTION TO VESTING

STEP

21

Vesting refers to the time when you have ownership of the money in your retirement plan. When you are vested, benefits must be paid to you, even if you leave the company years before your retirement. If you quit your job or are terminated before becoming vested, however, you can't collect any of the money set aside in your retirement fund. If you return to a former employer after a "break in service" or working somewhere else, you must be given credit for your prior service.

Many employers see vesting as a way to reward loyal employees for sticking with the company and as a way to keep employees on board. But under traditional defined benefit pensions, vesting by itself did not mean much in the way of benefits. Even an employee who worked 10 years for a company—say from age 22 to age 32—might have very little in the way of vested benefits, certainly not enough to turn down a good career opportunity.

The money you put in your 401(k) plan is vested immediately. Whenever you leave your employer, you have the right to take that money with you. But the money that your employer contributes—the company match or profit-sharing dollars—is a different category, controlled by the employer.

Your employer *may* provide immediate vesting on that money, too. But more likely, there is a vesting schedule that lays out how long you must work in order to get this money. Employers may provide vesting in one year or two years. But they are not permitted to establish vesting schedules that go beyond the maximums set forth in section 411 of the Internal Revenue Code. These guidelines permit two choices: five-year "cliff" vesting or three- to seven-year "graded" vesting.

Under cliff vesting, the employee is not vested in any of the employer contributions until he completes five years of service. Then he "falls off the cliff." He is immediately 100 percent vested in all employer contributions. If he leaves after that point, the money belongs to him. Under graded vesting, the employee becomes vested in 20 percent of employer contributions after three years, 40 percent after four years, 60 percent after five years, 80 percent after six years, and 100 percent in seven years.

It is probably not worth your while to stick with an employer to become vested in a traditional pension, particularly if you are young. Benefits in these pensions are heavily weighted toward older, higher-paid employees. If you've been working only five years, you may have earned a few hundred dollars to be paid 40-some years from now.

But with your 401(k) plan, it is quite easy to see what you gain by waiting until you're vested in the plan. For instance, suppose your employer matches 50 cents on the dollar of your contribution up to 6 percent of your salary. You earn $50,000 and contribute the 6 percent, or $3,000 per year. Your employer contributes $1,500 each year. After four years, your employer's contribution totals $6,000 plus the earnings on that money. If your employer provides for five-year vesting and you leave after four years, you leave that $6,000 on the table.

That shouldn't be enough money to persuade you to give up a great career move. But it's certainly enough to pay attention to. One of the great benefits of 401(k) plans is that they are portable. Even if you work for half a dozen different employers, you can still earn the same benefit that you might have earned working for just one. Check your company's vesting schedule and keep it in mind when planning your career.

CONSIDER THE QUALIFYING RULES

STEP
22

Employers who sponsor 401(k) plans must observe certain rules on when you can participate in the company's plan. They are permitted to impose two eligibility requirements. The first is called the "year of service requirement." It allows the employer to say that you must work for the company for a period of time before you are allowed to participate in the plan. But that time period cannot be more than one year.

The employer is also permitted to say that participants must be a certain age. But the maximum age the employer is permitted to specify is 21. In other words, your employer might say you must be 19 years old and work for the company for six months before you can contribute to the plan or that you must be 20 years old and work for the company for nine months. It may set any age and time considerations it likes *as long as* it is not more than one year and age 21.

Most of the confusion regarding this eligibility revolves around the year of service requirement as it relates to part-time employees, according to Jeffrey M. Miller, managing director at Putnam Investments and author of *The 401(k) Plan Management Handbook* (Irwin Professional Publishing, 1996).

A year of service is calculated as a 12-month period beginning on the first day of employment during which an employee works at least 1,000 hours, which is roughly half time. If an employee begins work on January 1 but does not work 1,000 hours by December 31, a new period begins again on January 1.

So an employee who continues to work part-time, just less than half time, or fewer than 1,000 hours a year, need not be covered by the 401(k) plan. Once an employee satisfies the minimum age and service requirements, though, he or she must be permitted to participate in the plan at the earliest of the following dates: either the first day of the plan year that begins after he has become eligible, or six months after the date on which he has become eligible.

Once an employee qualifies for participation, he may ask the employer to withhold a certain portion of his salary to be contributed to the 401(k) retirement plan. These are the pretax contributions that 401(k) plans are best known for. A 401(k) plan is actually part of a profit-sharing or stock-bonus plan that includes what is called a cash or deferred arrangement, or CODA. Remember the bonus plans that were the precursor of the modern 401(k)? Like them, the 401(k) permits the employee to ask the employer to defer a portion of his salary rather than giving it to him in cash. Many 401(k) plans also allow employees to contribute additional after-tax money that will earn interest on an after-tax basis.

In addition, most plans provide for an employer match, which must be completely nondiscriminatory. For instance, the employer might contribute 50 cents for every dollar contributed by an employee (totaling up to 4 percent of that person's pay). Finally, the employer may decide to make profit-sharing contributions. These are separate from the match and are based on the company's profitability and laid out in a formula. The 401(k) or CODA portion of the plan is only the elective salary deferral, Miller says. But people often use '401(k)' to refer to the whole plan.

So once an employee qualifies for participation in the company's 401(k) plan, contributions can come from four sources. The first and most common is employee pretax contributions, which the employee asks the employer to withhold from pay and to contribute to the plan. Second is employee after-tax contributions. Third and fourth, the employer may make matching contributions as well as discretionary profit-sharing contributions.

CHECK THE HARDSHIP
WITHDRAWAL RULES

STEP

23

With all the advantages of a 401(k) plan, why would anyone who is eligible pass one up? Surveys show that many employees simply don't understand how the plan works. But the main reason that employees don't contribute is because they don't want to lock their money up until retirement. All of us have many demands on our money. Some of them so pressing it's hard to see a way to squeeze out savings for the future. Setting some aside for retirement is admirable, but many employees feel they simply can't spare a dime.

Indeed, the money you put in your 401(k) plan is locked up. The regulations say that the pretax money you contribute cannot be distributed until one of these things happens: you reach age 59½; you leave the company; you become disabled; you die; the plan is terminated; or the employer that sponsors the plan is sold.

Employers realize that this inflexibility is a key hurdle to participation for many employees—particularly younger employees and those who are lower paid. So many employers have done what they can to make the money more accessible. As you know by now, there are many different categories of contributions. And there are a few exceptions to these tough rules. One is the hardship withdrawal, which outlines circumstances under which you are permitted to withdraw money from your plan.

Your plan is not required to provide for hardship withdrawals. If it does, it must adhere to the government's rules for them. It is the employer's responsibility to determine whether you in fact have a pressing financial need, or what the Internal Revenue Service calls "an immediate and heavy financial need." Your employer must also be satisfied that you have used your other resources and that a withdrawal from your 401(k) is necessary to fulfill that need.

There are just four needs that might make you eligible for a hardship withdrawal. They include:

◆ **Medical expenses** for you, your spouse, or your dependents;

◆ **Tuition and other fees** for the coming year of college for you, your spouse, or your dependents;

◆ **Money for a down payment** on your principal residence;

◆ **Money to prevent eviction** from or foreclosure on your principal home.

Of course, just because you are buying a home or going to college doesn't mean you qualify for a hardship withdrawal. You must have exhausted every other means of paying for these needs, including taking a loan from your 401(k). You should be prepared to have to fully document your financial need to your employer.

The hardship withdrawal is probably not looking too attractive to you now. But wait, there's more. Once you've cleared all these hurdles, and you get the money from your plan, you must pay tax on it as well as a 10 percent penalty for early withdrawal. And you will be barred from making contributions to your plan for one year.

Clearly, then, a hardship withdrawal is a last resort. Taking a loan from your plan is far more attractive than making a hardship withdrawal *(see* **STEP 28***)*. Most plans allow you to take a loan for any reason, with no questions asked. There is no tax due on the money. And you pay yourself interest, which goes into your 401(k) account.

READ THE SUMMARY
PLAN DESCRIPTION

STEP 24 Under ERISA, the major law governing pensions, each 401(k) plan administrator is required to file a summary plan description with the U.S. Department of Labor. Your employer is also required under ERISA to make the summary plan description available to plan participants. Each 401(k) participant must receive a copy of this booklet, which describes the plan in simple language, no more than 90 days after becoming a plan participant.

Your employer must provide an updated booklet every five years which includes all amendments and other changes to the plan. As Jeffrey M. Miller, managing director at Putnam Investments, notes in his book, *The 401(k) Plan Management Handbook*, many plan sponsors provide only what is legally required in this document, making for pretty dry reading. Some, though, have chosen to use it as a basic communications tool, beefing up the information required by the government to convey much additional information about the plan.

However your employer uses it, the booklet is one source of information that *must* be provided to you. It has to relate certain basic information in a manner that can be understood by the average participant. It is required to include technical information that you might need, such as the names of the trustee and administrator, and it must outline your legal rights.

Although you probably will not sit down with this document to read it cover to cover, you should know what it contains and keep it in a safe place with the other information about your 401(k) plan. Things the plan must include, according to Miller, are shown in the box at right.

SUMMARY PLAN DESCRIPTIONS

◆ **The plan's name.**
◆ **The employer's name and address.**
◆ **An employer identification number or EIN.** This is similar to your own Social Security number and it identifies your employer with the government.
◆ **Plan number.**
◆ **Type of plan.** A 401(k) plan is a defined contribution plan.
◆ **Type of administration.**
◆ **Name, address, and telephone number of the plan administrator.**
◆ **Identity of the plan's lawyer.**
◆ **Eligibility requirements.**
◆ **A statement that describes the plan's benefits for beneficiaries,** called joint and survivor benefits.
◆ **A statement describing vesting provisions.**
◆ **The name, title, and address of the plan's trustee.**
◆ **A statement that outlines provisions in collective bargaining agreements that might pertain to the plan.**
◆ **The plan's fiscal year.**
◆ **Sources of contributions and the method used to calculate the amount of these contributions.**
◆ **The plan's termination provisions.**
◆ **Claim and remedy procedures for participants.**
◆ **A statement of the ERISA rights of participants.**

CHECK INTO PLAN SAFETY

STEP

25

As the money in 401(k) plans has mushroomed over the past decade, many participants have asked questions about plan safety. A couple of years ago, there was a rash of stories in the press about employers who dipped into 401(k) accounts to pay their own bills and others who simply kept the money they withheld from employee paychecks and used it for their own purposes.

That's certainly a frightening thought. It would be more than enough to make you reconsider your 401(k). But it is something that happened at a very few, small employers. The chances that it will happen to you are *very* remote. Most employers are more than eager to follow all the rules. The contributions you make to a 401(k) plan are held in a trust. Your employer cannot touch that money. Nor can his creditors if he files for bankruptcy. The people and companies that have decision-making authority over the plan are fiduciaries, which means they must always act on behalf of the plan in an informed, prudent manner.

Each plan has a trustee who has responsibility for collecting the money, investing it, and paying it out. The plan also has an administrator or record keeper who keeps track of money coming in and checks for compliance with various government regulations. You can learn more about the people and institutions responsible for safeguarding your 401(k) money in the summary plan document. If you have any reason to question the security of your company's plan, you should read this document carefully. You can also check with the plan's custodian to make certain that the money you have contributed is safely deposited in your account.

Although the chance that your employer will steal the money is practically nonexistent, there is no specific federal guarantee that every dollar you put into a 401(k) plan will be there when you're ready to take it out. If you choose investments poorly, you could lose money. Ditto if you buy and sell investments at the wrong time. Even if the investments in your plan are good ones, you could be a loser if you buy stock mutual funds at a market peak and sell when the market tumbles.

In contrast, benefits from a traditional pension, or a defined benefit plan, are guaranteed by a federal agency called the Pension Benefit Guaranty Corporation. Employers pay an annual premium rate per employee to cover the PBGC insurance. Then, if a plan is terminated, the PBGC pays a basic level of benefits to employees who were covered by the plan. But you already know that 401(k) plans work differently. You are responsible for contributing to the plan and for picking good investments. The balance in your plan ultimately depends on how well you do this. It is your employer's responsibility to keep your contributions safe. And your employer is legally responsible for offering good investment choices and for supervising your money in the plan.

Those employers who elect to follow rules put in place by the Labor Department and effective January 1, 1994, must offer at least three distinctly different choices, each of which has a different level of risk. They must also provide you with educational materials and the opportunity to move your money between the different options at least once a quarter. Most employers are moving toward compliance with these rules, even though they are not mandatory. The rules are designed to provide you with the investment options and the tools you need to make sound choices. Capitalizing on them is your responsibility.

PART

3

HOW TO
Get In and Get Out

OU SHOULD GET INTO your company's 401(k) plan. Period. Okay, so you're 26 years old, and this is the first time you've had two nickels to rub together. Saving for retirement *is* boring.

Forget about retirement for a moment. Think about your life and your dreams. What do you want to accomplish in your career? Your financial life? You'll never reach those goals unless you save some money. There's no simpler way to save than by having it taken out of your paycheck before you get your hands on it. And there's no better return than the 50 percent you're likely to get from your employer's match before you even invest a penny. That means you put in $1, and your employer adds 50 cents. Then you decide where to invest the $1.50.

So get started. Even if you don't have enough information to choose investments yet, join the plan and put the money into a money market fund until you've done some more research. Do *not* procrastinate. That is the only way you can lose money in this deal. Once you've gotten started, there are some places you can go for additional information.

One of the reasons many people give for failing to contribute to a 401(k) is that the money will be locked up too long. If that's a concern for you, you'll want to know about the rules for tapping into the money when you need it. There are a number of ways to get access to your money, including 401(k) loans, which you may be able to make with a phone call. So find out how to get in—and how you can get out, when you have to. And then make sure you join the plan.

GET HELP FROM
HUMAN RESOURCES

STEP

26

Today you are expected to take respon-sibility for your retirement. The good news is that there is plenty of informa-tion available to help you. "It's up to you now to learn about your 401(k) plan," says Wendy Rhodes, a partner at Hewitt Associates, employee benefits consultants in Lincolnshire, Illinois. "But you can collect a barrel full of stuff to help you if you just take the initiative."

The first step is to identify the contact person for your 401(k) information. If your employer has a human resources department, start there. Many employers are hiring consultants like Hewitt to perform this task. Or they are asking the mutual fund company that provides the funds to do all the communications and education as well. So you may have a real person in your human resources department to talk with. Or you might deal with someone over the phone by dial-ing an 800 number. When you find the right source, Rhodes suggests that you ask these questions:

◆ **Are workshops available?** "More and more compa-nies are offering financial planning workshops for 401(k) participants," Rhodes says. "Many of them are held on the weekends or in the evening so you can bring your spouse along."

◆ **Is anything available on the Internet?** Some compa-nies have posted 401(k) information on the Net, Rhodes says. Others use consultants, like Hewitt, to build a site that can be used by their employees. For example, those who use the Hewitt site can use their password to look up their account balance and to buy and sell mutual funds.

◆ **Does the company have an Intranet site with 401(k) information?** Many companies are using their own networks to provide information to employees.

◆ **Is anything available to help project retirement needs?** Most plan sponsors have some type of modeling tool—usually computer-based—that helps you project your account balance over time. It might be a piece of software for your personal computer or it might be an on-line service or a part of the company's computer network. Be sure to ask if there is a user's guide to lead you through it.

◆ **Are there any simplified forms available?** Financial information can be intimidating. That's why IDG Books Worldwide developed its well-known series of books for "dummies," as in *Mutual Funds for Dummies*. Even the Internal Revenue Service came up with a short form for taxes.

Rhodes says many employers are beginning to respond to complaints that information is inaccessible by offering basic information. "They used to say: 'Look it up in the summary plan description,'" she says, referring to the official plan document. "But now they're developing easier-to-use materials." For example, one client asked Hewitt to develop one-page sheets that respond to a single common 401(k) question such as, "What funds are available?" or "How do I make a loan?" "We call them 'pizza sheets,'" Rhodes says. "You can get only the tomato or only the cheese."

◆ **Is there an employee newsletter?**

◆ **What other resources are available?** Companies take their responsibility to educate employees seriously. Many reprint and distribute articles from magazines that they feel might be helpful to employees, says Christine Seltz, a principal at Hewitt. "It wouldn't be unusual for a company to buy books and distribute them to employees, either," she says. Companies are continually upgrading the educational material, too. "If you haven't checked for five years, you'll probably be surprised at the new resources available now," Seltz says.

CHECK THE EMPLOYER MATCH

STEP 27 If you've been reading this book straight through, you remember that when Ted Benna designed the first 401(k) plan in 1981, what set it apart from a run-of-the-mill savings plan was that the employer offered a match for employees who made a contribution. The match is the magic. Without it, many employees would still contribute to receive tax advantages. But it is the match that guarantees you a return on your money that you cannot get anywhere else.

The math on that is pretty simple. Say you contribute $3,000 to your 401(k) plan. Your employer kicks in $1,500. That's a 50 percent return on your money before you've made any investment at all. A number of surveys by the major benefits consulting firms in the mid to late 1990s showed that most 401(k) savings plan sponsors provide a match—about 88 percent, according to Hewitt Associates, consultants in Lincolnshire, Illinois. Those companies who are changing their plans—and tinkering with the match—are generally increasing it and making it more generous.

You'll want to know what other plans offer and compare yours to a benchmark. The most common type of employer matching contribution is a 50 cent per $1 match up to a specified percent of pay. More than one-third of employers (36 percent) provide that match, according to Hewitt. Most common of all is 50 cents per $1 contribution up to 6 percent of pay. A number of plans provide a graded match beginning at $1 per $1 of contribution for, say, up to 2 percent of pay then 50 cents per $1 for the next 4 percent. So if your plan provides 50 cents on the dollar up to 6 percent of pay—or better—you know that it is a good one. Certainly you will want to contribute the full 6 percent of your pay. That means if you earn $75,000, you contribute $4,500 to get the full match.

Your employer kicks in an additional $2,250.

Some plans offer a match based on company performance, which might rest on profitability, sales, or earnings. That can be a particularly appealing formula for a small business. Consider how the Homer D. Bronson Co., a maker of industrial hinges, set up its 401(k) plan to do double duty. Like other employers, Bronson wanted to help employees focus on saving money for retirement. But the company also wanted to increase productivity and enhance its competitive edge in specialty hinge manufacturing, where it is one of three players.

In 1994, Bronson, which employs about 60 people, had just passed rigorous quality standards to receive certification from the International Standards Organization. To maintain the certification, Bronson must be audited each year. "It is very unusual for a small firm to get this certification," says Walter Schuppe, Bronson's chief financial officer. "It is strategically important to our business that we maintain it." In fact, with the new certification, Bronson won a major new account—Ford Motor Co.

Because Bronson wanted its 401(k) plan to emphasize the importance of the certification, the company devised an incentive-based match. "We said the company would match a portion of the first 4 percent of employee contributions," Schuppe says. "That portion would vary from 10 percent to 50 percent depending on how well we meet certain strategic objectives." The plan was set up on January 1, 1995, with three employee goals: safety, quality, and client service. The company promised to match 25 percent of the first 4 percent of salary for the first six months and then measure how well employees had performed in meeting these objectives and increase or decrease the match. When performance was evaluated on June 30, the company had passed its certification audit for the year and the company match was raised.

CHECK OUT LOAN PROVISIONS

STEP

28

The easiest way to tap into your 401(k) money is with a plan loan. More than three-quarters (81 percent) of 401(k) plans have loan provisions, according to a 1995 study by Hewitt Associates. In most cases, you can use the money for whatever you like—to make a down payment on a home, to buy a car, to take a vacation, or to satisfy just about any other need you have for ready cash.

There are several advantages to tapping your 401(k) for a loan rather than going to a bank. First off, you qualify for a loan simply by having money in the plan. Second, the interest you pay goes into your retirement account rather than to the bank. Although most of the rules governing plan loans are set by individual employers, the loans are also affected by some Department of Labor rules and some rules established by the Internal Revenue Service. For example, to avoid being taxed on the money, employees can borrow no more than 50 percent of the money in their plan up to a maximum of $50,000. The money must be repaid within five years unless it is a loan for a home, in which case the term is set by the employer. The most common term for a 401(k) home loan is 10 years, but some can run up to 30 years.

Although the employer sets the interest rate, the Department of Labor prohibits loans offering a below-market interest rate. In other words, your employer must charge you roughly the same as a bank would charge consumers. As a result, most employers tie their interest rate to the prime rate, the base rate on corporate loans at large money-center banks. So you can expect to pay one or two percentage points above that. Many plans also charge loan processing and administrative fees.

All of this makes a 401(k) loan sound like a no-lose

proposition. That's not quite true. First, you should know that most plans do not allow you to continue your repayment schedule if you leave the company. That means you must pay back the outstanding balance if you leave for whatever reason—whether you quit or are dismissed. If you do not pay back the entire balance, it will be considered a taxable distribution and you must pay tax and a 10 percent penalty on it that year. There's also the "opportunity cost," which means that your money will not be earning a market rate of return while you have it on loan.

There's another snag, too, one that I hadn't thought of until I read "Just Call Them 'Sucker Loans,'" by Lynn Brenner in *Bloomberg Personal* magazine. Brenner points out that there is a hidden cost to 401(k) loans because you borrow pretax money, spend it, and pay it back with after-tax dollars. Then, when you retire, you pay tax a second time on those same dollars. Brenner provides this example: you borrow $10,000 from your 401(k) for five years at 9.25 percent interest. Your repayments, including interest, will total $12,529 in after-tax dollars.

A taxpayer in the 30 percent bracket would need $17,897 before tax to repay that amount. So your taxes on the loan repayment total $5,369. If you're in the same bracket at retirement, you'll pay another $3,759 in tax on that $12,529. So taxes on the $10,000 loan total $9,128. Which doesn't mean that a 401(k) loan is out of the question. It's your money and you should tap it if you need it for an important opportunity in your life. But I wouldn't put an expensive vacation or paying off credit card debt in that category. What is an important opportunity? That's up to you. Starting a business, perhaps. Or adopting a child. Making a transition. But don't forget that you must be prepared to pay the loan back. You might also want to compare a 401(k) loan and a home equity loan before you make a decision.

PAY ATTENTION TO
BENEFICIARY DESIGNATION

STEP 29

Financial planners like Stuart Kessler in New York, who is chairman of the American Institute of Certified Public Accountants, say that clients make some of their biggest mistakes in naming beneficiaries. He suggests to clients that they name a spouse as beneficiary and children as contingent beneficiaries during their working years.

Once you retire and roll the money into an Individual Retirement Account, the rules become more complex. Seymour Goldberg, who specializes in retirement account issues, says he finds that clients often do not state clearly how children are to share in an IRA. For instance, a client might name his two children, John Smith and Mary Smith, as beneficiaries. Under that arrangement, if John Smith dies before the account owner, Mary Smith will get half the account and the other half will be paid into the estate, Goldberg says. But usually that is not what the account owner intended.

Instead, he suggests that clients who want the money shared equally between their children name the children "issue per stirpes," which means the children share equally. If one child dies, that child's share would go to his or her children. Goldberg says he finds that this, in fact, is what most parents intend to do and that they are surprised to learn that that will not necessarily happen if they simply name the children. If the institution that holds the account doesn't permit the "per stirpes" designation, Goldberg puts an asterisk by the name of each child with a footnote that says, "if this child dies, this share goes to his or her children."

Sometimes a client doesn't list all the intended beneficiaries simply because the form doesn't have enough lines, Goldberg says, not realizing the legal implications of such an oversight. Even if the account owner has painstakingly listed each beneficiary properly, the custodian may eliminate some of the paperwork in the computer. "A number of institutions can't code it properly on their computers," he says. "So even if you do it the right way and then you call the institution two years later, you find out that they destroyed your rider." In that case, Goldberg says, he sometimes advises the client to move the account. "We threaten them with taking the money away if they can't do it properly," he says.

For example, Goldberg recently had two cases where clients died and the brokerage firm couldn't find the form that designated the widow as beneficiary of the individual retirement account. In the first case, the IRA contained $80,000. The widow was permitted to roll it over into her own IRA because she was the sole beneficiary of the estate and the sole executrix. Goldberg was able to cite an Internal Revenue Service private letter ruling that permits a rollover under those circumstances.

In the other case, the widow inherited an IRA with $200,000. But here there were also some trusts involved as beneficiaries, so she was not the sole beneficiary. Because the beneficiary form was lost, the $200,000 was dumped into the estate and became immediately taxable. "They were crying about it," Goldberg says. "But there was nothing that they could do."

Now Goldberg is advising all clients to write once every five years or so to their IRA custodian to ask for a copy of the beneficiary form. If the custodian merges, he puts a note on his calendar to write to the merged firm to make certain that the beneficiary form survived the merger. If it's lost, it's a simple matter to provide a new one, as long as he makes certain to do it before the IRA owner dies.

WATCH OUT FOR A HAND-BACK

STEP

30

Federal laws dictate that 401(k) plans cannot discriminate unfairly in favor of high-income employees. If the plan is found to be discriminatory, it can be disqualified, which means it loses its tax benefits. To prove that a plan does not discriminate, the sponsor must complete a series of tests that the industry refers to as ADP —for annual deferral percentage—tests. This language simply means looking at the contributions made by the higher-paid group as a whole and the lower-paid group as a whole and comparing them.

The plan must pass the test 12 months after the close of the plan year, which is generally December 31. But there is an interim deadline of two and a half months after the end of the year, usually March 15. So a plan administrator typically tests the plan early in the year. If it fails the test, contributions are returned to certain highly compensated employees. These contributions become taxable to the employee.

Beginning in 1998, the highly compensated group that receives the refunds will change. "Some people will begin to get refunds in 1998 who never got them before," says Carl Mleziva, a consultant at Hewitt Associates, benefits consultants in Lincolnshire, Illinois. So it pays to understand how this arcane rule works.

In order to conduct the antidiscrimination test, the plan administrator splits the employees into two groups: the highly compensated and the non–highly compensated. The Small Business Job Protection Act of 1996 raised the dividing line between these two groups from $66,000 to $80,000. The administrator then determines how much the lower-paid group— those under $80,000—contribute to the plan, on average. Let's say it's 2 percent. That means the higher-paid group can contribute no more than 4 percent, on average, because the spread generally cannot exceed 2 percentage points.

The 1996 law that raised the cutoff was a blessing for those who earn between $66,000 and $80,000. These employees faced the most severe restrictions under the old law, which limited those first who contributed the highest percentage of pay. So a $70,000 worker who contributed $5,000—or 7 percent of pay—was likely to see a portion of his contribution returned. But a $150,000 worker who contributed $7,500—or 5 percent of pay—was unlikely to face any limitation.

The 1996 law deemed that it is the worker with the highest dollar amount that will be cut back first, which seems only fair. For 1997, only the first $160,000 of compensation may be counted for purposes of retirement plan contributions. That means anyone with a salary of $160,000—and higher—who has been contributing the full $9,500 may see a partial handback of contributions in 1998. "Many companies have hundreds of people in this group," Mleziva says. "They've probably never gotten money back before."

There's another problem buried in this rule for employees just above the old $66,000 limit, Mleziva says. Most 401(k) plans sponsors worry a good deal about passing these discrimination tests. One solution used by many companies is to put in place a percentage limit on contributions for those in the upper-income group. "A lot of plans cap their highly paid contributions to make sure the plan won't fail," Mleziva says.

He estimates that about two-thirds of plans use some type of cap. "Some plans have not removed these caps even though the law has changed," he says. So an employee earning $68,000 might find that his employer has capped his contribution at 4 percent, for instance, even though the new law permits him to contribute to the full legal limit of $9,500. "You should check into this and make sure you're not being shortchanged," Mleziva says.

CONSIDER AFTER-TAX CONTRIBUTIONS

STEP 31 Many 401(k) plans—nearly half, according to Buck Consultants in Secaucus, New Jersey—permit after-tax contributions. That's certainly not as appealing as putting in money before it's taxed. But some employees should clearly consider it.

If you're not contributing as much as you can to your plan already, this is not for you. Your first goal is to max out on your pretax 401(k) contribution. For many people, that means the legal limit of $9,500 for 1997. But some employees—those whom the government considers highly compensated—are usually not permitted to contribute that much *(see* **STEP 20***)*. The plan might limit them to a certain percent of salary— say 5 percent. Some of these employees may qualify to make pretax contributions to a supplemental, non-qualified plan *(see* **STEP 32***)*. But for many of them, the only choice will be to make after-tax contributions.

Compare an after-tax 401(k) contribution to buying an annuity contract or contributing to a nondeductible IRA. All three of these investments are made with after-tax dollars. But earnings accumulate tax free until the money is withdrawn. The after-tax 401(k) has a couple of advantages over the other two, though.

The major disadvantage to a nondeductible IRA is that accounting can be a nightmare. You are responsible for keeping track of which money has been taxed, which has not and the earnings on each. With a 401(k) plan, the plan administrator takes care of this headache. The downside of an annuity contract (which is an investment purchased from an insurance company) is that it includes some underwriting—or insurance—costs that you must pay for. These cut into your investment earnings. An after-tax 401(k), on the other hand, has neither of these problems.

The after-tax money is generally easier to tap into than the pretax savings, as well. For example, when Ed Emerman, a public relations consultant in Princeton, New Jersey, left his former job to set up his own shop, his employer cut him a separate check for his after-tax savings. That money came in handy while he was getting started in his own business. (After-tax money is not eligible for rollover to an IRA.)

Many companies also let you tap into the money even while you're on the job, according to Ethan Kra, chief actuary for retirement services at William M. Mercer Inc., benefits consultants in New York. However, when you make a withdrawal of after-tax money that you contributed after January 1987, the Internal Revenue Service considers a portion of it to be taxable earnings, which are also subject to the 10 percent penalty if you are under age 59½. Say you've contributed $10,000 after-tax and it's earned $1,000. Of every dollar you withdraw, 10 cents will be taxable.

Many employers have supplemental executive retirement plans (or SERPs) that allow employees to contribute pretax dollars to an unsecured plan. But these are typically only for the company's top executives. So those employees who earn more than the $80,000 limit but too little to qualify for the supplemental plan are prime candidates to tuck a little savings away in after-tax contributions.

What about the new Roth IRA, available beginning in 1998? Advisers are still divided on its appeal for those in the early and middle stages of their working lives. Some say it beats a 401(k) because there is no tax, ever, when the money comes out. Others, like Steven Lockwood, a pension consultant in New York, consider it most valuable for those who want to leave the money in their estates and less valuable for those who will need to consume the money. Stay tuned.

LOOK CAREFULLY AT
SUPPLEMENTAL PLANS

STEP

32

Over the past several years, employers have been scrambling to set up supplemental pension plans for highly compensated employees because of new limits on regular pension plans. Even employees happy to be covered by the new plans, though, may get unpleasant surprises at retirement. These plans do not offer the same security or tax advantages as traditional plans.

Regular pension plans, including both defined benefit plans and 401(k) plans, are called "qualified plans" because they meet certain rules and receive special tax treatment. The company receives a deduction for any contribution, and employees do not pay any tax until they receive the benefit. Even when they retire, employees can roll the money into an individual retirement account and defer taxes.

Over the years, qualified plans have been cut back for upper-income employees to help bolster tax revenue. Many companies have tried to make up for lost benefits by setting up supplemental executive retirement plans, called SERPs or nonqualified plans. Today SERPs represent a portion of the promised retirement benefit for many employees.

Consider how that works for Universal Health Services, a company in King of Prussia, Pennsylvania, that owns and operates hospitals. Back when the Tax Reform Act of 1986 reduced the maximum an employee could put into a 401(k) plan from $30,000—or 25 percent of pay—to just $7,000, Universal Health set up a supplemental plan to allow employees to continue to contribute up to the old limits.

Over the years, the $7,000 figure has gradually risen—to $9,500 in 1997. But Universal Health capped upper-income employees—like doctors and administrators—at 6 percent of pay in the regular, qualified 401(k) plan in order to make certain the company would pass the nondiscrimination tests. The rest would go into the supplemental plan. The company matched 25 cents on the dollar up to the first 4 percent.

Then, in 1994, a new law capped the amount of salary that could be considered for qualified plans at $150,000, a figure that is indexed. That means a doctor who earns $250,000 can calculate his 401(k) contribution—and match—only on $150,000. So this doctor would lose part of the company match. Four percent of his actual salary is $10,000, providing him with a match of $2,500. But 4 percent of $150,000 is $6,000, so he would get only $1,500. "So now, for a select group, we are putting the company match in the nonqualified plan," says Nancy Kurtzman, the director of employee benefits.

Most employees think of their retirement benefit as one piece. They do not understand part of it may come from a secured, qualified plan and another portion from an unfunded, nonqualified plan. "Many people would be shocked to see that the overwhelming portion of their pension is coming from a SERP and only a small amount from the qualified plan," says Bill Mischell, managing director of the Princeton, New Jersey, office of Foster Higgins, benefits consultants.

There are two serious drawbacks to these plans. Supplemental plans are merely a promise to pay a benefit; the money for these benefits is not set aside or secured in any way. So the employee faces the risk that the employer cannot pay or that it reneges on the contract. These plans also lack tax advantages. When the money is paid to a retiree, a chunk off the top goes to taxes. The remainder cannot be shielded in a tax-deferred retirement account, meaning future earnings will be taxed as well.

LOOK FOR A WITHDRAWAL
LOOPHOLE

STEP

33

You know by now that there is a 10 percent penalty levied on retirement money that is withdrawn before you reach age 59½. But there are some exceptions to that rule.

Perhaps the most significant one allows employees who leave their companies at age 55 or older to take the money in corporate retirement plans penalty free. "If you actually worked on your 55th birthday and you separated from service one day later, you can take the money," says Ethan E. Kra, chief actuary for the retirement practice at William M. Mercer Inc., benefits consultants based in New York. "You could be fired, you could quit, or you could just walk out the door and not tell them where you're going. The reason is immaterial."

That may be a comfort for people in their fifties who consider their jobs tenuous. Even taking another job does not disqualify the penalty-free withdrawal. The ability to take the money at age 55 is independent of anything else you do.

This early payout, however, applies only to tax-qualified retirement plans, like 401(k)s and Keoghs, not to individual retirement accounts. Nor is it available for employees who quit working or retire before age 55. Suppose you work for a company where you qualify for early retirement after, say, 30 years of service. Maybe you've completed the 30 years at age 52. But if you leave then, your money will be locked up until age 59½. In other words, qualifying for early retirement from the company does not qualify you for the exemption.

Of course, any money withdrawn from tax-deferred accounts is subject to income tax. One way to minimize the income-tax bite is to take just a chunk of the money. "You could take out the piece you need to live on until 59½ and roll the balance over or draw down installments if your plan allows it," says Christine A. Seltz, a principal at Hewitt Associates in Lincolnshire, Illinois.

The other option for getting at retirement money without paying a penalty is what the Internal Revenue Service calls "annuitizing," or taking substantially equal payments based on life expectancy. This method is available for IRAs as well as qualified plans and can be used at any age.

To qualify, a participant must take substantially equal payments for five years or until age 59½, whichever comes later. There are three methods permitted by the IRS. With the first, calculations are based solely on life expectancy. The second includes a reasonable interest rate on the money as well as life expectancy. The third allows the use of an annuity table. The first produces the smallest annual payout; the third the largest. But the difference is only a few hundred dollars on a lump sum of $100,000 for a 50-year-old, according to Don Roberts, a spokesman for the IRS.

Of course, the older you are—and the more money you have—the better this method looks. A 47-year-old has a life expectancy of 35.9 years. Annuitizing a $100,000 balance by the simplest method would amount to annual payments of just $2,800. It's certainly not realistic to expect to support yourself on such a paltry amount.

But look how a few years and a few hundred thousand dollars changes the picture. A 52-year-old who begins annuitizing a $750,000 balance that is expected to grow at 6 percent a year could take out $50,624 a year until age 82, according to Kra. Leaving the money untouched is always the best option. But it also pays to know what your other options are.

CONSIDER GETTING MONEY OUT
THROUGH THE BACK DOOR

STEP

34

Am I really going to be so irresponsible as to tell you how to sneak your retirement money out of your plan so you can spend it? Lots of studies show that the majority of 401(k) plan participants already take the money and spend it when they change jobs. That fact is alarming to those who know that Americans don't save enough for retirement. It's alarming to me, too. But I don't think it's my job to try to save you from yourself.

You should have all the facts. That way you can decide how to use your money. You should save it for retirement. Definitely. But you are also entitled to have the flexibility permitted by the law. A little-known section of a July 1992 law to extend unemployment benefits for the jobless had important implications for 401(k) plan participants. This law includes relaxed guidelines for rollovers that may allow employees who stay on the job to roll portions of their retirement money into outside accounts and still protect their tax-deferred status.

This could be an important option for those who are unhappy with the investment options in their employer's retirement plan. For example, some 401(k) plans still provide only one option. Sometimes that is company stock. Investing in the stock of the company where you work is rarely a good idea. Rolling a portion of it into an IRA would allow you to diversify your retirement account.

The rollovers are available from any type of retirement plan that permits a voluntary withdrawal, including some 401(k) and profit-sharing plans, according to Howard J. Golden, a tax attorney at Kwasha Lipton, benefits consultants in Fort Lee, New Jersey. "I see a lot of plans that say you can come in twice a year and make a withdrawal," Golden says. Prior to 1993, the money would have been taxable. It might also have been subject to a 10 percent penalty. Under the 1992 law, it can be rolled over with no tax consequences. "This is a tremendous opportunity," Golden says. "Now I can go in every year, make a withdrawal, roll it over, and diversify my retirement money."

It could be important, too, for those who want to take some money out of their plan but who cannot qualify under the hardship withdrawal rules. Suppose you make an in-service withdrawal from your 401(k) plan and roll the money over into your IRA. Once it is in your IRA, you can take it out whenever you want, provided you pay tax and the 10 percent penalty. I am not encouraging people to spend their retirement dollars on a vacation. But remember that one of the goals of this book is to help you use your 401(k) to create financial freedom for yourself. It's possible that you might want to start your own business or do something else that will enhance your life long-term. In that case, this is an option for you.

To find out if you can get money from your 401(k) plan, read the summary plan description. Look for in-service withdrawals and go to your benefits administrator for details. Ethan Kra, chief actuary for retirement services at William M. Mercer, the New York–based benefits consulting firm, says that many plans allow the company match to be withdrawn if the money is "seasoned." That simply means that it has been in the plan for a while. "In many plans, the company match can come out after two years," Kra says. "There is a form to fill out. Sometimes you can even process it on the telephone."

What should you do with this information? Tuck it away in the back of your mind somewhere so that you remember you have an escape valve. One of the things that scares people about a 401(k) is that they feel they've lost access to the money.

BE CAREFUL WHEN
YOU CHANGE JOBS

STEP 35

There are a couple of things that might trip you up in a job change. First, you must repay any outstanding loan on your 401(k) when you leave your job. If you do not, the money is treated as a distribution and it becomes taxable.

Second, you must take care to make certain that the entire account does not become taxable. In 1992, Congress imposed a 20 percent withholding tax on lump-sum retirement distributions that are paid directly to employees who change jobs, retire, or are laid off. The law, effective January 1, 1993, provides that employees who take their retirement money in a lump sum when they leave their job will receive only 80 percent, with the other 20 percent withheld for tax. Prior to 1993, 401(k) participants could take a check for the entire amount and defer all taxes if they rolled it over within 60 days to an Individual Retirement Account.

There are still several ways to avoid the tax:

◆ **Have your employer roll the money directly into an IRA.** If you decide to do this, set up a separate IRA, called a conduit IRA, to receive the money. That preserves your right to roll the money into another employer's plan later. That might be desirable because IRA money is not eligible for such favorable tax treatment as forward averaging, nor can it be borrowed. Both are possible with money in employer-sponsored plans.

◆ **Leave the money in your employer's plan.** This, too, will preserve your options.

◆ **Begin making periodic withdrawals from the plan, based on your life expectancy.** This option, which is called annuitizing, is available no matter what your age. You must pay tax on the money as you receive it, but you avoid a 10 percent penalty on premature withdrawals otherwise assessed if you are under age 59½. You must continue making the withdrawals for five years or until 59½, whichever is later.

◆ **Transfer the money directly to your new employer's plan.** This will not be an option for everyone. Many companies have a one-year waiting period.

Many people who lose their jobs worry that they will need the money from their retirement plans to live on. They are hesitant to have an employer make a direct transfer to an IRA. The law provides that if they take the money in a check—less the 20 percent—they can still roll it over to an IRA and receive a full refund of the withheld portion when they file tax returns for the year.

But that is only true if the total amount, including what was withheld, is deposited. Say, for example, you receive $40,000 from a $50,000 distribution, with $10,000 withheld. You would get a full refund if you took the $40,000, came up with $10,000 on your own, and put the total into an IRA within 60 days.

But if you roll over just the $40,000, you get only a partial refund. You will be taxed on the $10,000 and you will be assessed a 10 percent penalty for early withdrawal ($1,000) if you are under 59½. State taxes might also be due. By the time you discover this, it may be too late. "People who are less sophisticated about rollovers will take the check and discover too late that they can't raise the money," says Ethan E. Kra, chief actuary for retirement at William M. Mercer Inc.

If you lose your job and are uncertain about what to do, you would be much better off asking your employer to roll the money into an IRA. If you find that you must have it to live on, you can withdraw a chunk of it—even the very next day—and you are no further behind. Your goal should be to leave as much of it as possible in the IRA.

COORDINATE WITH YOUR SPOUSE

STEP

36

As if we don't each have enough money hangups and psychological obstacles to making good investments, now we have to try to reach agreement with a spouse? Indeed, deciding how to manage retirement benefits and allocate both dollars and investment options between spouses is a complex issue—one that could keep a team of psychologists busy for some time.

But it is important for couples to face this issue. Legally, a pension—and that includes 401(k) plans—belongs only to the participant in the plan. There are some loaded issues here. Coordinating your benefits makes some assumption about the longevity of your relationship. It's important for each spouse to feel that he or she is getting a fair shake in retirement dollars. That means putting aside money in each spouse's name even though it may not be possible to put the same amount aside for each spouse because of different types of retirement plans and different levels of compensation.

While you should aim for equity in the retirement dollars you put aside for each spouse, try to squeeze the most you can from the two plans. Although couples seem to be increasingly adept at making the most of their health insurance plans by picking the best from each spouse's coverage, I'm not sure the same strategy has been applied to 401(k) plans. Here are some issues to consider:

◆ **Match.** If you cannot afford to fully fund both spouses' 401(k) plans, be certain to at least capture the employer match in each one.

◆ **Vesting.** Pay attention to vesting, which refers to the time it takes before you actually own the employer match. If you leave before you are vested, you leave the match behind *(see* **STEP 21***)*.

◆ **Investments.** It is in the investment options that

couples have the opportunity to do some real coordination. Chances are each spouse's plan has limited choices. You may as well make the best of what each plan has to offer, provided, of course, that you see eye to eye on investments.

An investment portfolio should include a large-company U.S. stock fund as the core. If one of the two plans offers an index fund like the Vanguard Index 500 Trust, that's the ideal candidate. You also need a good small-company fund, an international fund, and perhaps a small exposure to emerging markets. It makes good sense to pick the best of the funds from each plan to build a retirement portfolio without overlaps. Still, I think it's critical that each spouse feel good about the selections in his or her own plan. So if Joe, the husband, has a great emerging markets fund but he just can't stomach that kind of volatility, I suggest that he pass it by.

A retirement plan is often a couple's biggest asset. If the couple divorces, the pension goes to the one who owns it. It can be split between the two partners only if the court issues a domestic relations order and the administrator of the plan "qualifies" the order, or makes certain that it meets the plan's requirements. This qualified domestic relations order, or QDRO, splits the retirement plan according to the couple's agreement.

QDROs were authorized by the Retirement Equity Act of 1984, which addressed spousal rights to a pension. The act became effective on January 1, 1985. Prior to that date, it was possible to split pension assets in divorce. But a court order was directed at the spouse with the pension, rather than at the pension plan itself. For example, the husband might be told by the court that once he began to receive a monthly pension—perhaps 15 years in the future—he should send half to his former wife. But if he died before retirement, the wife received nothing.

PART

4

Investing It

F OR MANY AMERICANS TODAY, a 401(k) plan is the first brush with the investment world. You may be just out of college, starting your first job, and here you are confronted with the task of picking mutual funds. Or you might be at mid-life and you've just joined a small employer that offers you a 401(k) plan—and the daunting task of investing it. It is intimidating indeed to choose investments that will play such a large role in determining your financial future.

Look at it like this. Investing is no longer optional. Twenty years ago, most Americans did not invest. They saved what they could and made do on that, help from families, and what they got from Social Security. Today everyone must invest. You must invest if you are to reach for your dreams, if you are to have the life you want. You must invest in case you lose your job or become divorced or widowed or want to educate your children. And you must invest to have the money to do the things you want to do in retirement.

Look at your 401(k) plan as an opportunity to learn as you go about investing. With a 401(k) plan, you can start small, make regular systematic investments, and get lots of information from your employer about the investment options in your plan. Remember, successful investing requires a plan and a strategy. Do not start until you have one. Learn about the basics. Be disciplined. When you develop your plan, stick with it through thick and thin. Don't get sidetracked by the "hot funds" and the investment of the moment. Anyone can learn enough to become a good investor. It's not rocket science. It requires the same sort of discipline as playing golf, practicing the violin, becoming a good cook.

STRETCH YOUR NOTION OF RISK

STEP

37

Before you invest your first dollar in your 401(k) plan, you must think about risk. Investing is risky. So is not investing. If you think that risk simply means that you might lose the dollar you have in your hand, you need to broaden your thinking. If you are too conservative, you risk losing new opportunities, losing your chance for a better life.

We will lay out the various types of investment risk in the next several pages. But the most basic risk most investors face is not an academic one but an emotional one: The *fear* that the money they invest will decline in value, even temporarily. A decline in the value of an investment makes many people feel both foolish and anxious. When these people think about risk, it means one simple thing: What is the risk to my principal? If I invest $10,000, is there any chance that my money will ever be worth less than $10,000? Can some of it disappear in some mysterious way? Could it be worth just $9,500 the following day?

If the answer to that question is yes, that's the end of the discussion. These people claim they have a low risk tolerance and they move on in search of another investment. Their choices are limited to bank certificates of deposit, Treasury bills, and money market funds. Unfortunately, unless you are wealthy to begin with, you will not earn enough in these "safe" investments to accomplish your goals. The less money you have, the more important it is for you to take some prudent risks. If your risk tolerance is too low for your own financial good, you must do something to increase it.

Think for a moment about the way you approach risk in other aspects of your life. Many people avoid investment risk chiefly because they lack knowledge about investments. Yet they shoulder huge financial risks in other areas. Getting married, having children, buying a house, changing jobs, starting your own business, moving: all of these carry enormous financial risk. Chances are good that you've done at least one of them. How did you make your decision? How did you make peace with it? You probably learned as much as you could about your prospective mate or your new job and then took the leap.

Learning more about investing is certain to help you feel more comfortable. So get educated. Learn to distinguish between different levels of risk, too. Just because an investment is risky doesn't mean it's good. Some risky investments are just plain foolish. And some people who sell them are looking to make a quick buck at your expense.

Risk and reward go hand in hand. That's one of the first principles of risk. Concentrating on one stock or one segment of the market is risky. It can also be extremely rewarding. So with a bigger potential reward goes the possibility of loss. For example, a mutual fund that invests in just one sector of the market is riskier than one that buys stocks more broadly, across different industries. If you had invested in a mutual fund that buys health care stocks in 1990, you might have doubled your money in a year. But if you made the same investment in 1992 instead, you might have lost 25 percent of your money in a year.

Remember, too, that time is on your side. Time horizon is one of the biggest factors in determining risk tolerance. If you have 10 or 20 or 30 years to invest your money, you can afford to be a big risk-taker. Because you are investing your 401(k) money for retirement, you have time to let it grow. For you, inflation is the biggest risk. Inflation means that the dollars you put away will be worth only pennies when you plan to spend them unless you invest them to grow at more than the pace of inflation.

TAKE A QUICK TEST

STEP 38

Life is about risk. Creating the life you want for yourself requires risk taking. Here are some questions to get you thinking about how you take risk in all parts of your life:

1 You and your spouse are ready to have a child. Both spouses work. But the husband's company announces coming layoffs. You would:
  - **a.** proceed full steam ahead; you're not getting any younger
  - **b.** figure that if the husband were to be laid off, he could perform child care duties while thinking about his next career move
  - **c.** put your family plans on hold for a year while the two of you get the lay of the land
  - **d.** reconsider having a family; life is too uncertain.

2 Your friend takes you to an early morning sale at a nearby clothing outlet. The prices are great, but you can't try anything on and you can't return it. You:
  - **a.** go for broke, buying five suits that you figure cost half what you would pay in a department store
  - **b.** choose one $500 item. You saw the same piece of clothing for $1,000 and you're willing to bet that you can alter it if it doesn't fit
  - **c.** buy a couple of low-priced items figuring that you'll just lose a little if they don't work out
  - **d.** spend two hours writing down sizes, prices, and brand names. You plan to go to the local department store and try these items on so that you can come back and buy them, knowing that they will fit.

3 After you make an investment, you typically feel:
  - **a.** thrilled
  - **b.** satisfied
  - **c.** confused
  - **d.** regretful.

4 It's time to plan your vacation. You:

   a. take off on a mystery tour where the destination isn't
   revealed until you're en route

   b. discover a small ad in the newspaper for a 50-percent-
   off charter flight to Thailand. You mail in your deposit
   and delight in your good fortune

   c. call a trusted travel agent to suggest two or three
   places that he knows you will like and then pick the
   most economical of the lot

   d. you don't have to plan because you always vacation at
   the same spot; you know it will be comfortable.

5 When faced with a major financial decision, you:

   a. flip a coin

   b. go with your gut

   c. research the options

   d. call each of your friends and ask for advice

   e. agonize.

**6 You think your boss is brilliant, but with him in
charge, you're never going to get anywhere. Then he
decides to start his own business and invites you to
come along as his No. 2. You:**

   a. go with him for a pay cut and a share of the company

   b. demand a higher salary instead of equity in the company

   c. stay where you are and hope to get his job.

If you picked the first answer to each of these six
questions, you are adventuresome indeed—perhaps
too much so. Be careful when picking investments not
to go overboard. If you picked the final answer to each
question, you may sometimes feel virtually paralyzed
when making financial decisions. See what you can do
to loosen up your thinking a bit. In any case, use these
questions to get you thinking about how you
approach risk and whether it's working for you in
investing—and in your life. We must all take prudent
risks in order to improve the quality of our lives. In
sports they say, no pain, no gain.

SCORE YOUR WHEREWITHAL

STEP 39 Each of us has some feelings about risk-taking and a general tolerance—or intolerance—for risk. Some studies suggest that we are born with an attitude toward risk taking. But your financial circumstances affect the risk you can take, too. If you are young and can set your money aside for a long time, you can afford to be very aggressive. Knowledge, too, can increase your capacity for risk taking.

1 If your age is: GIVE YOURSELF
    a. under 30   **5 points**
    b. over 30 and under 40   **4 points**
    c. over 50 and under 62   **3 points**
    d. between 62 and 65   **2 points**
    e. over 65   **1 point**

2 Your current income is:
    a. under $30,000   **1 point**
    b. between $30,000 and $50,000   **2 points**
    c. between $50,000 and $75,000   **3 points**
    d. between $75,000 and $125,000   **4 points**
    e. over $125,000   **5 points**

3 If your current investment assets are:
    a. under $5,000   **1 point**
    b. between $5,000 and $10,000   **2 points**
    c. between $10,000 and $50,000   **3 points**
    d. between $50,000 and $100,000   **4 points**
    e. more than $100,000   **5 points**

4 If your major investment goals are:
    a. zero to two years away   **1 point**
    b. two to five years away   **2 points**
    c. five to 10 years away   **3 points**
    d. more than l0 years away   **4 points**

5 What is your future earning power?
    a. keep pace with inflation if I'm lucky   **1 point**
    b. promotions and pay increases should keep

me a few points ahead of inflation **2 points**

c. far exceed inflation; big bucks ahead **4 points**

d. if you expect an inheritance or some other
big chunk of money **5 points**

6 Pick one:

a. I never save or invest **1 point**

b. I do my best to tuck away a few dollars
here and there **2 points**

c. I save regularly **3 points**

d. I put aside 5 percent of my income no
matter what **5 points**

7 Give yourself 1 point for each thing you do :

a. skim the financial pages from time to time

b. read the daily financial pages

c. keep abreast of daily markets

d. subscribe to at least one personal finance magazine

e. watch investment and financial programs on TV

f. subscribe to an investment newsletter

8 Pick one:

a. I am a knowledgeable investor, able to explain concepts such as standard deviation **5 points**

b. I use only mutual funds but am well versed
in the types available and how they work **4 points**

c. I have a grasp of the basics such as how the
stock and bond markets work **2 points**

d. I hate financial discussions and avoid them
at all costs **0 points**

If you picked up 25 points or more, you have substantial capacity for risk including both investment
knowledge and financial wherewithal. If you scored 18
to 24, you are in a position to take moderate risk. If you
scored 17 or below, be careful. You need to build up
some assets and some knowledge before tackling more
aggressive investments. It is well worth the effort. When
you feel comfortable with risk and can move from conservative to more aggressive investments, you should be
able to get an extra 2 or 3 percent a year.

LEARN THE RISK BASICS

STEP
40

You know you must invest. But when you invest, you *do* face special risks to your money that you should understand. Here are the most common ones:

◆ **RISK: Inflation, the general and continual increase in the prices of all the things you need to buy, such as food, housing, clothing, and medical care.** When you are investing for a long term goal, like retirement, inflation risk means that the dollars you stash away may be worth just pennies when you're ready to spend them in retirement. You risk losing your money to inflation if you don't invest at all or if the investments you choose don't earn enough to keep pace with inflation, which averages about 3 percent a year over a long period of time. There have been periods, like the early '80s, when inflation reached 12 percent and others, like the early '90s, when it was actually under 2 percent a year.

ANTIDOTE: Find investments that keep pace with inflation or—better yet—that beat it. When top financial planners build a portfolio for a client, they base the projected return on what they will get *after* inflation.

◆ **RISK: Rising or falling interest rates, which cause the price of many investments to rise or fall suddenly.** Bonds are hardest hit by changes in interest rates. The longer the maturity of the bond, the bigger the impact.

ANTIDOTE: Don't buy and hold long-term bonds. They are suitable for investors who want to bet that interest rates will fall. Other investors should use short and intermediate term bonds with maturities of less than 10 years.

◆ **RISK: Default by a borrower or issuer of bonds.** Credit or default risk is the chance that a borrower won't repay. When you buy a bond, you are lending money to the issuer. The greater the credit risk, the greater the interest rate a borrower or issuer of securities must pay. That's why high-yield or "junk bonds" carry the highest interest rates.

ANTIDOTE: Check the credit quality of bonds or bond mutual funds you buy. If you have very low risk tolerance, stick with investment-grade corporate bonds (AAA, AA, A, or BBB) or buy government bonds.

◆ **RISK: Lost opportunity.** Opportunity risk is the risk that you will tie up your money in a so-so investment and lose the chance to put it into something with real growth potential. Investors who buy long-term bonds or certificates of deposit face this risk. If you buy long-term bonds and rates go up, you have locked in a lower rate.

ANTIDOTE: Limit your exposure by diversifying your assets.

◆ **RISK: Concentration—or too many eggs in one basket.** Portfolios with many investments carry less risk than those with only a few because the diversification reduces the effects of losses or gains on any particular investment.

ANTIDOTE: Diversify.

◆ **RISK: That you won't be able to *reinvest* your earnings at the same rate next month or next year.** If you put $10,000 in a bond that pays 7 percent interest, you will earn $700 a year. But if rates drop, you will not be able to reinvest your $700 at 7 percent.

ANTIDOTE: None.

◆ **RISK: Lack of marketability.** Marketability risk is the chance that there will be no ready market for your investment if you want to sell in a hurry.

ANTIDOTE: Use mutual funds, which can be bought and sold any business day.

You still face the risk that your fund shares will be worth less because of changes in the markets, of course.

THINK ABOUT CORRELATION

STEP

41

Before you begin to invest your 401(k) money, think about some of the concepts that guide professional investors. It goes without saying that a professional wrings emotion out of the investment equation. Investing is a bit of science and a bit of art—but it is never emotional.

Part of the reason a professional can be so objective is because he uses investment tools, some of which you should use, too. One of them is what investors call *correlation*. Correlation measures the way two securities— or two mutual funds—perform relative to one another. The reason you buy more than one investment is to diversify. But if both your investments do exactly the same thing, you haven't achieved your goal.

Let's assume that you will use mutual funds for your 401(k) plan. What you don't want is two mutual funds that move in lockstep. If two investments move in tandem, professionals refer to that as a perfect positive correlation of 100 percent, or a correlation coefficient of +1.0.

Two investments with a correlation of -1.0 would provide a perfect negative correlation. That would be great if you could find them. Those two investments would provide a perfectly diversified portfolio. Unfortunately, there are no two investments with a perfect negative correlation.

But investors are always on the lookout for investments that behave in different ways in the same environment because such investments decrease the risk in a portfolio. That's because when one investment takes a dive, another one performs well. "What you want is one investment that zigs when another zags," says Don Phillips, president of Morningstar Mutual Funds.

All correlation measures fall somewhere between the perfect positive of +1.0 and the perfect negative of -1.0. Investment professionals consider investments with a correlation higher than .75 to be highly correlated—and a poor choice for diversification.

Many novice investors buy a group of well-known funds believing they have achieved good diversification. But large funds are likely to hold the same well-known stocks that are touted by research reports. The bigger a fund is, the more difficult it is for it to find investments that are off the beaten path. Tiny companies don't have much impact on a giant fund like the $63 billion Magellan Fund. So big funds gravitate to the same big companies.

To measure correlation, we compare one fund to another. Consider how these six funds correlated with the Janus Fund over a five-year period:

Fund	Correlation
Fidelity Contrafund	.96
Fidelity Growth & Income	.95
Vanguard Index 500	.95
Vanguard Wellington	.92
Fidelity Magellan	.89
Twentieth Century Ultra	.89

Clearly, in terms of diversification, none of these funds would make a particularly good match with Janus. Nor would owning all of them give you much more diversification than owning Janus alone. It is of particular interest to see the high correlation with the Vanguard Index 500 fund. Vanguard 500 follows the movements of the Standard & Poor's 500-stock index. What this high correlation shows you is that Janus—and the other funds as well—probably hold chiefly large-company U.S. stocks. That means they will behave a lot like the big-company U.S. stock market. You would not want more than one of them in your portfolio. Instead, you should match up a large-company U.S. fund with funds that perform well when large-company stocks do poorly.

LOOK AT WHAT
THE PROS USE

STEP
42

Professional investors use academic tools to measure risk and to analyze and compare the performance of different mutual funds. The most common measurement of risk—and perhaps most useful to individual investors—is *standard deviation*, which shows how far the return of a mutual fund might be expected to deviate from its average return, based on its history. Think of a bell curve with the average—or mean—in the middle, which is a wide band above and below the mean. A standard deviation is an equal number of returns above and below the average. Statistics tell us that we can expect the returns of a fund to fall within one standard deviation from the mean two-thirds of the time. And returns can be expected to fall within two standard deviations 95 percent of the time.

For instance, let's say the average, or mean, return for Fund X over a period of three years is 10 percent. The standard deviation is also 10. So one standard deviation encompasses returns from 0 percent to 20 percent; two standard deviations range from -10 to 30 percent. If you looked at such a fund, you might say that there is almost no chance that you will lose more than 10 percent or gain more than 30 percent in a year with this fund, based on its history. If the same fund had a standard deviation of 15, the range of your expected returns would fall between -20 percent and 40 percent.

Let's look quickly at the three tools of Modern Portfolio Theory. *Beta* measures risk or the volatility of a fund relative to the market; *alpha* attempts to measure the value added—or subtracted—by a portfolio manager by showing the performance of a fund relative to the risk it took. And *r-squared* attempts to show how much confidence you can put in a fund's beta and alpha by showing you how similar the fund is to the market. We'll start at the bottom.

R-squared shows the percentage of movement in a particular security or mutual fund that is explained by the movement in an index, ranging from 0 to 100. So a stock or fund that moves in tandem with the S&P 500 would have an R-squared of 100, because 100 percent of its movement is explained by the movement of the S&P.

So it is that the Vanguard Index 500 has an r-squared of 100. All of its movement is attributed to changes in the index itself. But the T. Rowe Price Japan fund has an r-squared of just 2 to the S&P because this fund invests in Japan. A better fit for it is the Morgan Stanley Capital Index–Pacific. Here it has an r-squared of 73, according to Morningstar.

Beta measures the volatility of a fund by comparing its return to the return of a benchmark, which has a beta of 1.0. A fund with a beta of 1.0 tracks the movement of the index exactly. A fund with a beta of 1.25 has 25 percent more volatility. That means you can expect it to rise 25 percent more in an up market and sink 25 percent more in a down market. A fund with a beta of .75 is less volatile than the market. You can expect it to get a return 25 percent lower than the overall market when the market goes up and to lose 25 percent less when the market falls.

Beta is neither good nor bad. But it is meaningful only if the r-squared is high. For instance, the T. Rowe Price Japan fund has a beta of .23. But its r-squared of 2 shows that its movements don't correlate with the U.S. market. When measured against the Morgan Stanley Pacific index, it has a beta of .83.

Alpha is an attempt to measure the value a manager adds—or subtracts. A positive alpha implies the manager delivered more return than could be expected given the risk that he took. A negative alpha implies that the portfolio was not compensated for the risk.

DIVERSIFY

STEP

43

Asset allocation—or selecting the right mix of asset classes, such as international stocks, small-company stocks, large-company stocks, bonds—is the key to successful investing. Combining different asset classes allows you to include assets that seem risky by themselves—like small stocks or emerging markets—and still create a portfolio that has low volatility because of the correlation between these assets and the way they offset each other.

Here are some of the key asset classes you will want to consider for your portfolio:

CASH EQUIVALENTS

Money market funds and Treasury bills

BONDS

Short-term bonds (3- to 5-year maturities)

Intermediate-term bonds (5- to 10-year maturities)

U.S. SMALL-COMPANY STOCKS

Growth

Value

Micro (invests in tiny companies)

U.S. LARGE-COMPANY STOCKS

Core, like the S&P 500 stock index

Growth

Value

Yield, such as equity income fund

INTERNATIONAL

Developed countries

Emerging markets

INFLATION HEDGES

Natural resources funds

Real estate funds

Energy funds

SPECIALTY

Sector funds

For investors with a long time horizon, stocks should represent the bulk of the portfolio. To determine how much, think again about your risk tolerance, or your ability to deal with volatility. Stocks have the highest average annual return over time. But they follow a bumpy road to get there. Adding bonds and/or cash to your portfolio cushions the ride. A portfolio of 60 percent stocks and 40 percent bonds is a typical mix.

But what if you've got the tolerance for risk and you want to go for the highest return? Many professional investors put 100 percent of their personal portfolios in stocks. Yet some studies show there is little extra to be gained with the final 15 percent. In other words, a long-term portfolio that is 85 percent in stocks and 15 percent in short-term bonds or cash might be ideal because it provides market returns with a small cushion against market volatility.

Whatever portion you decide to put in stocks should be spread across the stock groups listed above. Some investors neglect to put money into large, established U.S. companies because they rightly believe the real growth will come from small, undiscovered companies or from those companies just getting established in developing countries. But investors who pursued that strategy in 1995 and 1996 were sorely disappointed. Large-company U.S. stocks raced ahead, gaining 37 percent in 1995 and another 23 percent in 1996, leaving small-company funds, international, and emerging markets in the dust. Other investors stick to the established companies, reasoning that they represent less risk. That group was handed a disappointment in 1997 when small companies took the lead, turning in a spectacular performance in the second and third quarters. The shifting fortunes of these different categories of stocks prove the benefit of including each of them. Do not wait until a particular asset class takes off to get on the bandwagon. If you do, you could miss out on most of the upswing.

INVEST IN STOCKS

STEP 44 Studying the stock market can be a life-time job—and it is for many professionals. Even if you are just a novice, you probably understand that *no one* really knows when the market will go up—or why—and when it might head down. There are hundreds of theories about what moves the market and how to invest. Perhaps you've heard of the Elliott Wave Theory or investing in the Dogs of the Dow.

Yet if you followed the market on October 27, 1997, when it plummeted by 554 points and then gained 337 points the following day, it was clear the movements of the stock market are largely a mystery, even to those who follow it regularly.

Don't make the mistake of thinking that you must understand all of this stuff in order to be an investor. Think of it like peeling an onion. There are layers and layers of information about the market. The number of layers you want to peel off—and the amount of time you want to spend peeling—should determine what kind of investor you will be.

If investing doesn't interest you and you don't want to spend much time on it, just peel off the first layer. You need to know that stocks represent equity in a company. When you buy stock, you become a part owner of that business. Your fortunes become those of the companies you own. You share in their prosperity and your investment suffers during their hard times.

Most companies—particularly the large ones—pay dividends on their common stock. If the company has a great year, it may raise the dividend and the share price may go up. If the company gets sued—or announces that its earnings will not be as high as anticipated—the share price might nosedive. Because the fortunes of a single company are difficult for a novice to predict, most investors choose to invest in mutual funds and choose a money manager to do the analysis and pick the companies.

Professionals debate endlessly about the efficiency of the market. An "efficient" market would quickly correct inaccuracies in the pricing of securities. So if a stock was priced too low, investors would snap it up. If it was too high, they would sell. An efficient market would constantly right itself like a finely calibrated scale. The more efficient the market, the fewer the opportunities to make money, of course. But there are plenty of pockets of inefficiency. For example, not all investors have the same information about the companies that are traded. That creates inefficiencies.

But the chief reason for inefficiency is the vagaries of investor psychology. Richard H. Thaler, professor of economics at the University of Chicago's graduate school of business, puts it this way: If everyone investing in the market were totally rational, no stock would ever be bought and sold. If someone wanted to sell 100 shares of IBM, you wouldn't buy it precisely because he wanted to sell.

But not everyone investing in the market is rational. Professionals believe that individual investors like you and me are particularly irrational. That's why they have devised many contrarian tools to help them invest in a manner that is *opposite* to what we do.

The key to investing in stocks is to avoid making irrational decisions. That's it. If you want to peel just one layer off the onion, simply resolve that you will not be irrational; that you will not second-guess yourself and pull out of the market. Thaler says the perfect investor resembles Rip Van Winkle. You invest and then go to sleep for 20 years. Whenever you think about selling, remember that. For you, index funds are the investment of choice *(see* **STEP 45***)*. If you want to peel another layer, read on.

CONSIDER THE CASE
FOR INDEX FUNDS

STEP
45

If you are a mathematician or an engineer, you're going to love this. If you're an artist or an English major, it's worth your trouble to see it through. An index fund—or a passively managed fund—invests in all the stocks that make up a particular index or in a sampling of those stocks. Once invested, it's passive, simply holding the stocks. There is no active manager to pick and choose among a variety of stocks and to collect fees for doing that. Likewise, there are few trading costs. A good index fund moves up and down with the market. The Vanguard Index Trust charges just one-fifth of 1 percent in expenses. That compares to 1.43 percent for the average actively managed stock fund.

Passive management grew out of the work in efficient market theory of a number of economists in the 1960s. John C. Bogle, chairman of the Vanguard Group, explains efficient market theory this way in his book *Bogle on Mutual Funds* (Irwin, 1994):

◆ **All investors together own the entire stock market.** Passive investors as a group will match the gross return of the overall market because they are invested in all the stocks. So active investors, as a group, can do no better. They, too, must simply match the market.

◆ **Because the fees and transaction costs incurred by the passive investors are much lower than those paid by active investors and both groups get the same gross returns, then it follows that passive investors will get the higher *net* returns.** Indeed, active managers must beat the market by 2 percentage points just to come out *even* after paying expenses.

Yes, I hear you saying, but active managers as a group include some good managers and some bad managers. You are going to choose the good ones—

the ones that beat the average. Bogle concedes that there are excellent managers who outperform the average and mentions Warren Buffett, Peter Lynch, and John Neff. But, he says, "such extraordinary managers not only are few in number but are difficult to identify in advance."

Bogle cites academic studies that show that only two in five stock mutual funds outperform the market over time and only one in five does so once sales charges are taken into account. The performance of active managers is inconsistent and it is usually not the same ones who outperform from year to year.

Big institutional investors like pension funds immediately saw the merits of passive management. The first institutional index fund was opened in 1971 and billions of dollars poured into these funds throughout the 1970s. The first retail index fund, the Vanguard 500, was set up by Bogle in 1976 and its early success was much more limited. The indexing story lacked romance and passion—the two things that lure individual investors. But the fund began to grow in the late 1980s as individual investors grasped the logic of passive investing. Then—in 1995 and 1996— money poured into the fund, bringing it to number two in size and putting the index fund in the unlikely position of the "hot fund" of the year.

I suspect that much of this money was coming into the fund for the wrong reason; that many of the new shareholders did not understand that an index fund moves up and down with the index with a slight difference for expenses. They were not selecting the index fund for the mathematical reasons outlined by Bogle in his book. Instead, these were investors in search of the hot fund. They saw that the index 500 was outperforming in the bull markets of 1995 and 1996 and they wanted in on the action.

Be careful when you choose indexing. Buy the argument and then buy the index.

CONSIDER THE CASE
FOR ACTIVE FUNDS

STEP

46

Over the past decade, thousands of hours have been spent debating the merits of passive management—investing in a static portfolio that is usually designed to mimic a market index—versus active management—active security selection by a money manager. Most of these debates focus on the academic arguments for one versus the other. In fact, though, the issue is largely one of individual style.

I think Ross Levin, a financial planner from Minneapolis, said it best when he introduced a panel on active versus passive management at a financial planner conference in Palm Beach, Florida, in 1997. Levin said that he uses actively managed funds because he enjoys doing the research to find the funds. Active managers are more interesting to him and more interesting to his clients. "Active managers keep my clients interested and keep them in the investment game," Levin said. But he acknowledged that if he preferred passive management he would no doubt attract clients who preferred passive funds. "What I really think matters is that you believe in what you're doing and have passion for it," Levin said.

Intellectually, the argument for indexing is a strong one. I suspect most professionals accept it. Yet each and every one of them believes secretly that he will be the one to beat the odds.

Consider Professor Burton G. Malkiel, author of *A Random Walk Down Wall Street* and a great advocate of indexing. In his book, he explains that because the markets are efficient, most active managers fall behind the market index. Yet Malkiel uses active funds himself. He also argues that investing is fun. "A successful investor is generally a well-rounded individual who puts a natural curiosity and an intellectual interest to work to earn more money." That means picking active managers. Malkiel took it one step further in 1997 when he introduced his own actively managed mutual fund.

And Paul Samuelson, the Nobel laureate economist whose work was instrumental in the development of index funds, invests in Berkshire Hathaway, the company run by Warren Buffett, the best-known investor of our time. Even Vanguard's Bogle buys some actively managed funds.

There's really no contradiction here. As Malkiel says in his book, the fun of investing is to pit your intellect "against that of the vast investment community and to find yourself rewarded with an increase in assets." I think you could make the argument that, even if you did no better than the index—or did slightly worse—it could still make sense for you to use active managers if it helps you to learn about investing and to stay in the market. If that's so for you, you should consider active management. It should be perfectly clear to you at this point where you belong. If your eyes glaze over at the thought of reading *The Wall Street Journal*, stick to index funds. If you can't wait to tuck in with a cup of tea and *Outstanding Investor Digest: Perspectives and Activities of the Nation's Most Successful Money Managers*, you're going to be bored by index funds. Stick with active managers.

But index funds and active funds need not be mutually exclusive. Think of it as a continuum stretching from an investor who indexes his entire portfolio to one who uses index funds as a core and selects active funds to complement them to one— like Morningstar's president Don Phillips—who uses all active managers. Then think about where you fit on that continuum chiefly based on the passion you have for investing.

EXPLORE INVESTMENT STYLES

STEP 47 A decade ago, investors were advised to buy funds based on their objective, such as "aggressive growth" or "income" or "growth and income." But the labels were broad and confusing. Two aggressive growth funds were likely to pursue two entirely different strategies in search of growth.

As investors have grown more sophisticated, they've begun to look at funds based on the manager's investment style. By style, we mean chiefly two things: What size companies does the fund buy, and what method does it use to select them? You should keep investment style in mind as you invest your 401(k) portfolio as well.

The two key investment styles used by stock investors are value and growth. Value investors look for companies with a hidden value that is not reflected in the stock price. They certainly do that in a lot of different ways. The *Outstanding Investor Digest,* an excellent newsletter for hard-core investors, devotes 65-plus pages in each issue to exploring the ways investors like Warren Buffett of Berkshire Hathaway, Ron Baron of Baron Asset Fund, and Michael Price of Mutual Series analyze balance sheets in search of value.

Some might poke around in bankruptcy filings. Many look for companies that hold assets like real estate that could be sold for a gain. They look at comparable companies in the same industry to get an idea of the stock's potential. Most look for some catalyst, like a new chief executive, that might unlock the hidden value in the company. Many value investors like companies with a low price/earnings ratio. The p/e ratio shows the relationship of the stock price to earnings. It could be last year's earnings, this year's earnings, or projected earnings. Some also like companies that pay high dividends or that generate a lot of cash flow.

Growth investors don't care about any of this stuff. They believe that rapidly rising corporate earnings are the single most important thing driving stock prices. That's what they look for. Many of them don't care at all about high p/e ratios or other measures that seem to indicate that a company is overpriced by some traditional valuation. They might buy companies that are deeply in debt because they believe that they're growing so fast that they'll overcome the debt quickly.

Some growth managers are called *momentum* investors because they buy stocks based on earnings momentum—sometimes without any regard for the nature of the company's business or anything else. They might use a computer program, for instance, to look for "earnings surprises," or those companies that report earnings higher than the consensus of Wall Street estimates. Some growth managers claim they do not even know what business their companies are in.

Academics have done considerable research to try to determine which investment style is more successful—value or growth. What they've concluded is that they do well in different market environments. If you are using actively managed funds, you should include both investment styles.

Fortunately for you, Morningstar Mutual Funds began in 1997 to categorize funds based on investment style. In addition to value and growth styles, Morningstar looks at company size. There is a great deal of evidence to show that small companies have more growth potential over time than big, well-established companies. But small company stocks run in cycles and during many periods they are outperformed by large company stocks. So you should include both. That means a diversified portfolio would have a large company growth fund, a large company value fund, a small company growth fund, and a small company value fund for domestic stocks.

TAKE A LOOK AT
THE BOND MARKET

STEP

48

A bond is a loan. If you go to a bank to borrow money, the bank looks over your credit history and decides whether to offer you a loan. The banker also decides what interest rate you will pay. If your credit is immaculate, you may get a lower rate. If you are a bad risk, you probably won't get a loan at all. Instead, you will end up borrowing money wherever you can get it—and probably at a very high interest rate. When you take out the loan, you agree to pay a set rate of interest and to repay the loan over a specified period of time.

When a large institution wants to borrow money, it may go to a bank the same way you do to make a loan. Or it may decide instead to borrow from investors by issuing a bond. Part of that decision is based on the level of interest rates. If they are low, the institution might want to lock in the low rate for a long term, just like you do when you take out a mortgage on your home, by issuing a bond.

Bonds are the debt of corporations and government agencies. When you invest in a bond, you are making a loan to the bond's issuer. The issuer promises to pay you a set rate of interest, which is sometimes called the *coupon*. It also agrees to repay the principal at a specific time. (You probably repay your bank loan in installments. The issuer of a bond typically repays in a single lump sum at maturity.)

Your concerns as a bond investor should be the same as those of the bank that loans you money. First is the ability or willingness of the issuer to repay the money. Bonds are assigned letter grades by Moody's Investor Service and Standard & Poor's Corporation as well as other rating agencies that indicate their creditworthiness. These letter grades are akin to your personal credit history. They give the lender—in this case the bond investor—an objective evaluation of the institution's ability to repay.

The safest bonds are those issued by the U.S. government because they are backed by the full faith and credit—and the taxing power—of the government itself. Then come corporations with an AAA rating, ranging all the way down to those with a D rating, which means the issuer is in default, and those that are classified as NR because they have no rating.

The higher the credit rating, the lower the risk for the investor and the lower the interest rate or coupon that the institution will offer to pay on its bond. Bonds issued by companies with a low rating or no rating are called "high yield" or "junk" bonds. They offer the highest interest rate of all because the investor assumes a higher level of risk.

So one risk you face as a bondholder is credit risk—or the risk that the issuer will not repay. The second risk is interest rate risk, or the effect of a change in interest rates on your bond investment. Because the interest rate of your bond is locked in, the price of your bond—what you could sell it for on the open market—will fluctuate to reflect the change in interest rates. When interest rates rise, the price of the bond you hold falls.

If you buy a single bond, you are totally exposed to both credit risk and interest rate risk. Buying a bond mutual fund minimizes both those risks. The fund manager buys and sells bonds daily, spreading credit risk over a large number of issues. Because it is unlikely that all the companies whose bonds are in the portfolio will default, you gain protection from this diversification. Likewise, the fund manager adjusts the average maturity of the portfolio as interest rates change.

INVEST INTERNATIONALLY

STEP 49 Just one generation ago, U.S. stocks represented two-thirds of the value of all the stocks outstanding in the world. Today that statistic has neatly flip-flopped: Two-thirds of all stock value is to be found outside the U.S. Investing in this country alone is too limiting for investors today.

But investing overseas offers more than just variety. One of the best arguments for going abroad is that stock markets in different parts of the world tend to hit their peaks and valleys at different times because of different economic conditions. Remember that diversifying your portfolio so that one investment zigs when another zags is one of the best ways of decreasing risk and building wealth because gains in one asset will offset losses in another. "When you put somewhere between 30 to 40 percent of a U.S. portfolio in international stocks, you both increase the rate of return and decrease overall volatility," says Mark Holowesko, director of global equity research for the Templeton Funds in Nassau, the Bahamas.

Some researchers argue that this negative correlation between foreign and domestic markets has lessened as the world has become a global marketplace. But Laurence R. Smith, managing director at J.P. Morgan, says, "We continue to expect economic cycles to diverge. There is a lot of support for the idea that global diversification will continue to pay off."

Unfortunately, though, there is no clear-cut pattern showing that foreign investments do well at the very time when U.S. investors most need them—when the market here nosedives. Still, it is clear from looking at 10-year returns of the U.S. market compared to the Morgan Stanley Europe, Australia, New Zealand, Far East Index (EAFE) that investing both here and abroad provides diversification.

In an article in the November 1997 issue of *Bloomberg Personal,* Burton Malkiel, author of *A Random Walk Down Wall Street,* and economics professor at Princeton University, argues that the 21st century will see the rise of the emerging markets of the world. Malkiel points out that 85 percent of the world's population lives in developing countries from Eastern Asia to Latin America, and that growth in those areas is two to three times that of the Western world.

Four factors support continued rapid growth in those markets, Malkiel says. First is privatization. Production has soared with the coming of free markets. Second is the ready source of labor at low cost and a strong work ethic. Third, open trading systems will spur growth. And fourth, high savings rates in foreign countries will provide a source of investment capital.

A study by Malkiel and J. P. Mei for their new book, *Global Bargain Hunting,* found that a 10-year investment entirely in U.S. stocks produced a relatively low level of risk, but also a lower return than international stocks. Putting the same investment into foreign stocks increased both risk and return. The two found the highest return and the least risk could be produced by allocating 70 percent of the portfolio to U.S. stocks, as measured by the Standard & Poor's 500 stock index, and 30 percent to international stocks, represented by the Morgan Stanley Europe, Asia, and Far East Index (EAFE).

But adding emerging markets to the portfolio reduced the risk and increased the return further. The optimum portfolio in terms of risk/reward characteristics was 13 percent in emerging markets, 26 percent in developed foreign markets, and 61 percent in U.S. stocks. "As long as you add a widely diversified group of emerging-market stocks to a developed market portfolio, you will actually lower your risk and quite possibly increase your overall return," Malkiel says.

LOOK AT THE MONEY MARKETS

STEP

50

Time was when people referred to cash, they meant the coins jingling in their pockets or the bills squirreled away in the cookie jar. During the Great Depression of the 1930s, cash meant one thing: cold, hard currency that you could count on. It was something you could spend in the next 15 minutes if you wanted to. Even money in the bank wasn't cash in the 1930s. But after Franklin D. Roosevelt signed the Banking Act of 1933 and created the Federal Deposit Insurance Corporation, which put a government guarantee behind bank deposits, Americans gradually began to accept banks. Then bank accounts, too, became "cash."

But our definition of cash changed radically in the 1970s. "Cash" as we know it today was actually invented by Bruce Bent, who was casting about for a business idea. Bent hit upon a plan to collect money from depositers and loan it out to corporations at a slightly higher rate than what he paid depositors for it. So far, it sounds sort of like a bank. Yes, but Bent figured he could offer a higher interest rate because he didn't have the overhead of a bank. He quickly ran up against the Federal Reserve Board's Regulation Q, which imposed a 5.25 percent ceiling on the interest banks could pay on savings accounts. So Bent decided to use a mutual fund format rather than set himself up as a bank. His mutual fund would accept money from depositors and use it to make short-term loans to government and big corporations in the money markets, just like a bank did. But it would not be hampered by Regulation Q. Like other mutual funds, it would make money by charging depositors a management fee.

In November 1971, the Securities and Exchange Commission approved Bent's registration for the Reserve Fund, the first money market mutual fund. Money market mutual funds invest in short-term debt or short-term "paper," issued by the U.S. Treasury, state and local governments, banks, and large corporations. These loans are for very short terms, ranging from just overnight to perhaps 90 days. The SEC mandates that the average maturity of a money market portfolio by 120 days or less and that the fund invest only in the top two grades of debt as rated by Standard & Poor's Corp. or Moody's Investor Services. Because the investments made by the money market fund manager are so stable, these funds offer a fixed share price instead of one that fluctuates from day to day. So if you invest $1,000 in a money fund, you will own 1,000 shares. The share price remains at $1, so you will preserve your principal. The way you earn money is through the interest they pay: the interest rate is adjusted daily to reflect changing conditions in the money market.

The Reserve fund revolutionized the way America thought of cash because it offered instant access to money with same-day telephone redemptions. Although Bent invented the money market fund, he didn't have the field to himself for long. The big mutual fund companies quickly introduced their own funds with appealing twists like check writing, the ability to switch into other mutual funds in the family, and wire transfers to banks.

Today when investors talk about cash, they mean something entirely different from money in their pocket or even in a guaranteed bank certificate of deposit. When an investor says he is "in cash," he means he's not invested in the stock or bond markets. Instead, he's moved his money into a money market fund to earn short-term rates of interest. Perhaps he wants to stay liquid because of short-term needs for the money. Or maybe he's waiting for a good opportunity to buy. "Cash" still means that the money is safe, liquid, easy to get to. But few savvy investors consider the cookie jar a sensible place to keep it.

EXAMINE YOUR PLAN'S
INVESTMENT OPTIONS

STEP 51 When you decide to contribute money to your company's 401(k) plan, you will usually be given a choice of investments, some conservative and safe, some more aggressive and riskier. The number of investment options in the typical 401(k) plan is on the rise. The average number of options available in 1996 was 7.7, up from just four in 1990, according to a study by Foster Higgins, a benefits consulting firm. Unfortunately, more options doesn't necessarily mean better options. Offering numerous choices "has a lot of PR appeal," says Brian Ternoey, a principal in the Princeton, New Jersey, office of Foster Higgins. "But when you look back on it, a lot of these plans have been slapped together. There wasn't much investment planning involved."

That puts more of a burden on the participant to decide which options are good ones and which meet his needs. You can set up a 401(k) portfolio with just two choices, provided one is an investment in stocks and the other a fixed income investment such as a bond fund, a money market fund, or a guaranteed investment contract. The way you divide your money between them depends on your risk tolerance. You already know that stocks offer the best potential return. But they also have the most volatility, which means they can fluctuate enormously in value. If you don't mind that—and you consider yourself an aggressive investor—you might put 75 to 85 percent of your 401(k) money in a stock fund and the remaining 15 to 25 percent in a fixed income fund like a money market fund or bond fund.

When you invest in your 401(k) plan, though, you must go through two steps to pick investments. First, you must think in terms of the asset classes or categories that are right for you. Second, look at whether the choices in those categories are good ones. For example, you might want to invest in a U.S. small company fund. Yet, this is one of the most difficult fund categories to pick. If the small-cap fund in your plan has a poor record, you should avoid it. Perhaps you will have to invest in small caps outside your company plan.

But let's suppose for a moment that you had a plan like the one offered by Chrysler Corp., where you could choose from any stock or mutual fund you wanted in a self-directed account. I asked Harold Evensky, a respected financial planner and investment manager in Coral Gables, Florida, which asset classes he would use to set up model 401(k) portfolios if he had no restrictions. Here is his answer:

◆ short-term bonds
◆ medium-term bonds
◆ long-term bonds
◆ large-company stock index fund
◆ large-company value stock fund
◆ large-company growth stock fund
◆ small-company value stock fund
◆ small-company growth stock fund
◆ foreign stock fund investing in developed countries
◆ foreign stock fund investing in emerging markets

Evensky devised 14 different portfolios for investors with different risk profiles based on these asset classes *(see Part 8, "Sample Portfolios")*. Because he realizes that few plans offer such a wide range of options, he also developed portfolios based on just five asset classes: short-term bonds, long-term bonds, large-company stocks, small-company stocks, and international stocks. If you work for a large company, chances are good that you will have those options in your plan.

One of the challenges you have with your 401(k) plan is choosing investments from a limited menu. You must make do with the options you have. Not investing is not an option. But choosing just two or three funds is a viable solution.

THINK ABOUT THE BEAUTY
OF DOLLAR COST AVERAGING

STEP

52

Successful investing is all about discipline: discipline in buying and discipline in selling. The best way to discipline yourself is with a systematic investment program in which you make regular monthly or quarterly investments no matter what is happening in the market.

Investing in a 401(k) plan is the perfect way to do this. You decide at the beginning of the year how much you want deducted from your paycheck. And that amount is automatically invested based on your instructions at regular intervals throughout the year.

Making automatic investments at regular intervals allows you to take advantage of a "strategy" called dollar cost averaging. It's one of those jargony-sounding terms that has a very simple meaning: investing the same amount of money at regular intervals through thick and thin. Dollar cost averaging allows investors to avoid guessing whether the market is going up or down. The advantage to this method is that your dollars buy more shares when the price is down, fewer when the price goes up. That allows you to spread your risk, because you are paying varying prices for shares of the same fund. Studies show that investors who use dollar cost averaging tend to pay less per share over time than those who purchase shares in a lump sum.

Dollar cost averaging works particularly well when buying volatile funds because the same $100 investment buys more shares when the fund's price is down and fewer when it's up. When left to our own devices, most of us tend to do just the opposite: We buy a fund when it's "hot" and trading at its high and we dump it when the price sags.

This is how it works. Suppose your 401(k) plan offers a good small-company fund that appeals to you. But the sharp up and down swings in its price—or net asset value—scare you. Say you elected to put about 20 percent of your 401(k) contribution—or $100 a month—into that fund. To illustrate the point, we'll look at an extreme example. Let's suppose that in January, Small Fund is trading at $25 a share. You buy four shares. In February, it's trading at $20 and you buy five shares. Over the course of the year, the share price goes as low as $8—you buy 12½ shares that month—and as high as $25. At the end of the year, you've invested $1,200 and, in my example, you have 87 shares. So you've paid an average of $13.79 per share. Had you invested your entire $1,200 in January, you would have purchased just 48 shares. Assuming Small Fund is a good investment and that it climbs back to $25 and above, you will be much better off for having bought many of your shares when the fund was trading at a lower price.

Investment professionals—like financial planners—sometimes argue about dollar cost averaging. Some say that if you have a great deal of money and you plan to invest it in stocks, you should just get going. Because we know that the stock market provides the best return over time, "there's an argument to be made for getting on the stock line so you can start moving," says Eleanor Blayney, a planner in McLean, Virginia. However, planners like Blayney have also seen the studies that show that if they dump a lump sum into the market all at once, there is a 30 percent chance that they will experience a short-term loss. That is enough to convince most planners to use dollar cost averaging.

But with your 401(k) plan, you won't be making a decision about whether to dollar cost average. You simply sign up and indicate how much you want to contribute. That amount will be automatically deducted from your paycheck, and you will get the benefit of dollar cost averaging.

LOOK AT HOW
MUTUAL FUNDS WORK

STEP

53

Forty percent of American households own mutual funds. Yet surveys show that most Americans still do not know what a mutual fund is or how it works. A mutual fund pools the money of hundreds or thousands or even millions of different investors and invests it in stocks, bonds, money market instruments, and other securities. Each fund sets rules such as a minimum amount you can invest. The money you invest is pooled with that of all the other investors and used to purchase securities.

There are thousands of funds. Each one has a stated investment objective. It might be something like, "this fund seeks current income," which means the fund is designed for investors who need regular income from their investments. Or it might be "this fund seeks capital appreciation," which means it is designed for investors who hope for long-term growth in their money.

In order to accomplish the objective, the fund company hires a professional money manager to make investment decisions, trade securities, and accomplish what it is that the fund sets out to do. The way he plans to accomplish this is outlined in the prospectus.

Think of a mutual fund as a big pie cut into thin slices. Each slice is called a share. Each share is allotted a portion of the fund's gains, losses, and income. And each share is allotted a portion of the fund's expenses.

Investors decide how much to invest—$2,000 or $5,000 or $10,000—and they buy a specific number of shares. If a fund is trading at $10 per share, an investor who invests $1,000 will buy 100 shares. The share price of $10 is called a net asset value, or NAV.

Every day the mutual fund company calculates the value of all the assets in the portfolio. Then it deducts

expenses, which include management fees, administrative costs, advertising expenses, and servicing fees,
which are used to pay brokers and others who service
the account. The remaining assets are divided by the
number of shares outstanding to come up with the
value of a single share or the net asset value or NAV.

You can look up the NAV in the morning newspaper. A fund company is obligated to buy and sell
shares at the current price, or NAV, on every business
day, although some funds add sales charges or
redemption fees. Mutual funds pass on all their gains
or losses to the shareholders. The shareholders
receive two types of income from mutual fund investments: dividends and capital gains. And they pay taxes
on this income as if they owned the securities out-
right. A mutual fund is just that simple.

Mutual funds have numerous advantages for
investors. They provide professional management,
instant diversification, and convenience. They are also
easy to buy and sell. You can sell on any business day,
even if you own the funds in your 401(k) plan. The
trend is for 401(k) sponsors to offer daily trading.

Mutual funds also offer flexibility and variety. There
are more than 8,000 mutual funds offered by about
650 mutual fund groups or families, and the number
is constantly growing. You can pick from conservative,
blue-chip stock funds, funds that aim to provide
income with modest growth, or those that take big
risks in the search for capital gains. Of course, you
can't pick from all 8,000 mutual funds for your 401(k)
plan. And that's just as well. It is the job of your
employer to offer you a range of funds in your plan
from which you can construct a portfolio. A good plan
offers one fund in each of the important investment
categories or asset classes, such as large company U.S.
stocks and international stocks. Even though a mutual
fund offers diversification, you still need more than
one fund to provide a truly diversified portfolio.

WATCH THE EXPENSES

STEP

54

If there is a catch to 401(k) plans, it is this: they cost too much. Fees in 401(k) plans are roughly double what they should be, according to Adele Langie Heller, a retirement plan investment consultant with RogersCasey in Darien, Connecticut. And they're heading up from there. Employers are shifting these increasing fees onto employees. So it's time for plan participants to find out what they're paying and what they can do about it.

There are three basic cost components to a 401(k) plan, according to Timothy G. Murphy, a consultant at Hewitt Associates, benefits consultants in Lincolnshire, Illinois, who has written articles on this issue.

1 Investment management costs, or the cost of managing the money in the plan, which is expressed as a percent of assets. It seems logical for participants to pay this fee.

2 Trustee costs, which Murphy separates into custody charges and general processing fees. Services in this category—such as the cost of cutting a check for a loan—can be charged per activity. They should be, too. It makes sense for the person who requests the loan to pay for it rather than adding that cost to the overall plan.

3 Administration costs include record keeping and employee communication and education, as well as many of the fancy frills like voice response systems. I think you could argue that education is the employer's responsibility. But they're passing that cost on.

When a 401(k) plan uses mutual funds, many of these fees are wrapped into the mutual fund expense ratio and paid by the mutual fund investors. That's the money that is subtracted from mutual fund assets each year. It is expressed as a percent of assets—usually in basis points. A basis point is 1/100th of one percent. So an annual expense ratio of 1 percent might be expressed as 100 basis points.

You can look in the mutual fund prospectus to find the fund's expense ratio. Heller claims that a good large-company domestic stock fund should have an expense ratio in the neighborhood of 82 basis points, just as the plan at her employer, RogersCasey does. But the industry average is 128 basis points. A reasonable expense ratio for a bond fund might be 42 basis points, says Heller. The industry average is 78 basis points. And there are many 401(k) participants out there held captive in plans that charge much more. "There is real pillaging going on," says William McNabb, head of the institutional business at Vanguard Group in Valley Forge, Pennsylvania. "There are funds that charge 175 basis points. That's just egregious. Participants should scream."

Many fund companies are also adding 12(b)1 fees, which is a separate annual charge that comes out of the fund's assets. This fee is authorized by the SEC to pay for marketing and distribution expenses. In the case of 401(k) plans, the fund uses the extra fee to pay a consultant who puts together an alliance or group of funds to be offered in 401(k) plans. So participants are being forced to pay so the fund can get into other 401(k) markets. Reject high 12(b)1 fees. Better yet, reject all 12(b)1 fees.

Some small-company plans go even further. They use mutual funds with loads, or commissions. And they may add yet another layer of annual fees that are charged based on a percent of assets in the plan. That could be the last straw. If you are offered a plan where the employer contributes nothing in the way of a match, and you are losing 2 or 3 percent of your contribution each year to a combination of commission and fees, you'd be wise to explore other retirement options.

GET THE PROSPECTUS

STEP 55 Your employer is not legally required to provide you with the prospectus for mutual funds offered in your 401(k) plan, according to Frank Roque, an attorney at Hewitt Associates, benefits consultants in Lincolnshire, Illinois. That's because the 401(k) trust is the legal owner of the mutual fund shares, not the 401(k) plan participant. So the mutual fund company must provide the trust with the prospectus for each fund. "But the trust doesn't have to pass them on," Roque says. Still, Roque adds that most employers—more than half—do pass them on to participants nonetheless.

If yours is one of them, take a look at it. If not, get a copy for yourself. If your plan's mutual funds are sponsored by one of the retail mutual fund companies, like Fidelity, Putnam, Vanguard, or T. Rowe Price, you can get a copy by calling the company and asking for one.

A mutual fund prospectus can make for dull reading. But it's worth your effort to find out the fund's objectives, restrictions on the portfolio manager, fees, and other charges. Pay special attention to:

◆ **Summary of expenses.** Look here for the annual fund operating expenses, the cost of running the fund. These include the management fee, which covers salaries and administrative expenses, and the 12(b)1 fee, which covers marketing expenses. Most funds also have a category called "other expenses," which includes miscellaneous fees. The average expenses for a diversified U.S. stock fund are 1.43 percent of assets—which is high. See here how the fund compares.

Look, too, at the following example, which the company is required to provide, of what you would pay on a $1,000 investment assuming a 5 percent annual return and redemption at the end of the time period. Here's an example from the prospectus of one good no-load fund:

1 year	$10
3 years	$32
5 years	$56
10 years	$124

◆ **Financial history.** This shows up to 10 years of the fund's performance. Check to see if the fund has cut into net asset value to pay out dividends. Is the expense ratio declining over time or increasing? Is the portfolio turnover rate fairly steady and modest, for example, in the 50 percent range?

◆ **Investment objective.** This states where the manager will put most of his money. For example, "the fund will invest substantially all of its assets—but no less than 80 percent—in common stocks." How will the rest be invested? What other options does the manager have? Many funds now say, "The fund can invest up to 33 percent in foreign securities." You will also want to know whether the fund can use derivatives and how they can be used. A derivative is an instrument whose value is "derived" from the movement of a stock, interest rate, market index, or commodity such as wheat, sugar, or coffee. It typically relies on leverage to magnify the effect of price movements in the underlying security or commodity. The aggressive uses of derivatives get all the attention. But many derivatives are used to protect against big fluctuations in share price—for example, they might be used by funds that buy securities based in other currencies to hedge against swings in the dollar-exchange rate.

◆ **Performance.** Look at the fund's total return for the past 10 years, which is calculated according to Securities and Exchange Commission regulations. It will be compared with an index, usually the S&P index for a domestic stock fund. Don't expect it to beat the index every year. Instead, look for consistency. Check to see how the fund did in years when the S&P was down as well as in the S&P's best years. A smooth ride is important.

REBALANCE

Once you've thought through your risk tolerance, looked at asset classes, made your investment selections, and started your 401(k) contributions, is your work finished? Not quite. Now you must do two things that are seemingly contradictory. First, you must have the discipline to stick with your plan. Second, you must rebalance your investments once a year.

One of the keys to investment success is to avoid second-guessing yourself; to stick with the asset allocation you've made no matter what happens in the markets. So when you read that the stock market is getting too high, just let that roll off.

However, your asset allocation will grow out of balance on its own simply because of the cycles in the investment market. That's when you have to do something. Think of it as weeding a garden. You've selected the plants well, now you must control their growth. For many investors, this is the toughest part.

If you pick a winner and it takes off, chances are you feel proud of your investment prowess. Why prune it back? Because it's not giving the other investments a space in the sun. When you put together your portfolio, you selected different types of funds that would do well in different market climates. Left untended, your portfolio will grow toward the market sector with the best recent performance.

Consider this simplistic example. Suppose you have 50 percent in an S&P index fund, 25 percent in a small-cap fund, and 25 percent in an international fund. If the foreign markets that your international fund invests in doubled last year while U.S. stocks had a pretty miserable year, perhaps you now have 50 percent in international funds, 20 percent in the S&P index, and 30 percent in small-company funds (because they did better than the larger funds in our example).

It's tempting to stick with your winners. But it is this emotional attachment to investments that trips up most investors. If you understand market cycles, you know that what goes up comes down. International funds, too, will have their down cycles.

Rebalancing—if it is done rigorously and unemotionally—helps you to do what all investors want to do: buy low and sell high. It encourages making contrarian plays because you are selling the investments that have done well and buying those that have done poorly. In our example, the U.S. stocks will have their run-ups, too. If you rebalance, you will catch them before they start to move.

Consider what Brian Ternoey, a principal at Foster Higgins, benefits consultants in Princeton, New Jersey, did with his 401(k) portf io when his employer offered only two options: . stock fund and a guaranteed investment contract, or GIC. Ternoey, whose specialty is 401(k) management, knows that stocks have the best return over time. So he knows that a retirement portfolio should be chiefly in stocks. But he also knows that diversification is important. Ternoey put 75 percent in the stock fund and 25 percent in the GIC. Once a year, he rebalanced his portfolio. If stocks have had a good year and have grown to 85 percent, he sells off a bit, bringing the stock portion back to 75 percent. If they've had a bad year, he adds to the stock fund to bring his portfolio into line.

The key to rebalancing is to remove all emotion from it. Don't try to guess when it's time to sell one fund and buy another or to redirect your investments. That amounts to trying to time the market, which cannot be done successfully. Instead, pick a date, perhaps the first day of the year, and ruthlessly sell off the winners and add to the losers. Your 401(k) plan is the perfect place to do this because there are no tax consequences when you sell.

DON'T BUY COMPANY STOCK
OR LIFE INSURANCE

STEP 57 There are some investments that do not belong in your retirement plan. They include stock in your employer's company, insurance products, and municipal bonds. Many companies offer company stock as one of their 401(k) options. Do not choose it. You already have your livelihood tied up with your employer, who pays your salary and offers you employee benefits. You do not want to have your retirement tied to the fate of the same company. Think of what happened to employees at IBM in the early to mid 1990s. This was a company that had prided itself on never laying off an employee. And its stock was golden. But thousands of employees were forced out of Big Blue at the same time that the company's stock hit the skids.

What if your company matches your contribution with company stock? Take it, of course. You have nothing to lose by accepting a "free" gift.

Tax-advantaged investments like municipal bonds and life insurance products are not good retirement account vehicles either. Financing a retirement plan with pretax dollars is a big advantage for investors, who do not have to pay taxes until they make withdrawals. But buying a tax-advantaged investment within the plan provides no extra tax benefit. In this category are municipal bonds, whose income is free from federal income taxes, and life insurance policies, whose cash value grows tax deferred. The decision is more difficult if you have no choice. For example, participants in 403(b) plans may find that an annuity is their only option *(see Part 7, "403(b)s, 457 Plans, Etc.")*. In that case, you should weigh other factors such as the convenience of payroll deduction to invest for retirement and the attractiveness of the investments. But do pay careful attention to fees and expenses.

Insurers frequently urge people to buy a life insurance policy—or an annuity—inside a retirement plan, arguing that premiums can be paid with pretax money. "It's the only way you can buy life insurance with tax-deductible dollars," says Joyce V. Gordon, head of the pension division at Guardian Life. But Glenn Daily, a fee-only insurance adviser in New York, calls that advice misguided. "A retirement plan is the only way to buy mutual funds with tax-deductible dollars," he says, "and the return is a lot better" than with an insurance policy.

High fees are a drag on insurance returns, too. In a report for a city whose employees bought life insurance in a retirement plan, Ethan E. Kra, chief actuary for retirement services at William M. Mercer Inc., found that 100 percent of the first-year premiums went to sales costs and none went to investments.

Another negative is that the value of the death benefit, not the cash value, is imputed income. This value appears on an employee's W-2 form, and income taxes are owed each year. For that reason, insurance policies are disappearing from 401(k) plans, says Janet Shepherd, head of research for Hewitt Associates.

But annuities are not. An annuity is an insurance company product that offers tax-deferred buildup of earnings. Like insurance policies and municipal bonds, annuities have no place in retirement accounts. Fees on these products are high to provide for the life insurance guarantees that are wrapped into them.

Most retirement plans have a choice of investments. When you have a choice, keep it simple. Go for low-cost, no-frills basic mutual funds. Avoid your company's stock, municipal bonds, and insurance company products.

LOOK AT THE NEW
CAPITAL GAINS RATE

STEP
58
Does putting stocks in your retirement account still make sense with the new, lower capital gains rate? Yes, provided you have plenty of time to let them grow—at least 15 or 20 years.

When spreads widen between regular income tax and capital gains tax, investors look for ways to convert ordinary income to capital gains. Under the Taxpayer Relief Act of 1997, capital gains will fall to 18 percent for assets bought after December 31, 2000 and held for at least five years. That compares to a top rate of 39.6 percent for ordinary income—a substantial difference.

Capital gains are the profits you make when you sell an asset for more than you paid for it. They apply to gains in real estate, stocks, bonds—even a boat or a car—or any other piece of property that you own and sell for a gain. For income tax purposes, capital gains are separated from the ordinary income that you earn on your job or in your passbook account. The thinking here is that returns to capital should not be taxed like ordinary income and that much of a capital gain is simply a result of inflation.

For these reasons, capital gains have historically been taxed at a lower rate than regular income. For example, in 1980, capital gains were taxed at 20 percent while regular rates went as high as 70 percent. But for the last several years, the spread has been a narrow one. The Tax Reform Act of 1986 mandated that capital gains and regular income be taxed at the same rate—28 percent. In 1991, the spread opened a little with capital gains remaining at 28 percent and regular income rising to a maximum of 31 percent. In 1993, maximum tax rates rose again—to 39.6 percent—increasing the spread between capital gains and regular income tax. After May 7, 1997, long-term capital gains on assets held more than 18 months will be taxed at 20 percent with the rate falling to 18 percent in certain cases outlined above.

How can you play the spread? Some taxpayers put bonds in a tax-deferred account and stocks in a taxable account. That's because bonds pay regular income in the form of interest payments and that income can build up tax-free until the money is taken out of the account. They put stocks in a taxable account, reasoning that the gains will be taxed at the lower, capital gains rate. "It seems intuitive to put bonds in your retirement account where the income is tax deferred and to invest in stocks in a taxable account." says Steven Norwitz, a vice president at T. Rowe Price & Associates, the Baltimore-based mutual fund company.

Yet when Norwitz looked at the strategy, using the returns of stock and bond mutual funds over the past 20 years, he found that investors who put stocks in the tax-deferred account came out ahead, provided they could leave the account untouched for as long as 20 years. "The new law pushes out the required holding period," Norwitz says. "But it's still worthwhile." For investors in the 28 percent tax bracket at retirement, it took 11 years of holding the stocks in a retirement account to come out ahead of the investor who bought his stocks in a taxable account; at a 31 percent tax rate, it took 15 years; and at 36 percent, it took 20 years just to break even.

Norwitz attributes the somewhat surprising results to a number of factors. Stocks returned an average of 15.4 percent a year over the period, compared to 8.7 percent for bonds, which gave stocks a big push. Stocks also pay dividends, which are taxed as regular income. And when the stocks are held in a mutual fund, the fund pays out capital gains, which are taxed to shareholders in the taxable account.

PART

Preparing
FOR CHANGE

PLANNING AND SAVING well in advance are certainly critical for a successful retirement. Arguably, though, it is how you handle the actual transition from the full-time employer that sponsors your 401(k) plan to the next phase of your life that will make the biggest difference in your satisfaction and happiness.

Perhaps, for you, that step will indeed lead to retirement. More likely, though, you will be exchanging one kind of work for another. Please don't think that sounds dreary. Work is one of only a handful of essentials to a happy life—along with food, shelter, and love.

It's never too late to pursue your dreams through your work, either. Brendan Gill, the architect writer for the old-time *New Yorker,* picked 75 famous and not-so-famous "Late Bloomers," for his book of portraits by the same name. These are people who achieved self fulfillment, who realized the best of themselves, in the winter of their lives. "If the hour happens to be later than we may have wished, take heart!" Gill wrote. "So much more to be cherished is the bloom."

So what will *you* do in your post-corporate life? Whatever it is, make room for a passion. Perhaps you will turn a long-time hobby into a part-time business. Maybe you will have a second career. Your work need not be paid work to be satisfying. Maybe you hope to spend the bulk of your time with a theater or church group, scuba diving, studying French, or raising horses.

Whatever you will do, it will require careful planning—both financial and lifestyle planning. Here are some of the steps you should take to get the most out of this transition.

BE REALISTIC ABOUT
YOUR NEW LIFESTYLE

STEP

59

Financial planners say they are constantly amazed by clients who approach them at age 50—or 55 or even 65—and ask if they can retire even though they may have just $10,000 or $15,000 in the bank and no pension or other retirement income. "It's astounding," says Ginger Applegarth, a planner in Boston who finds that clients look her up after seeing her on CNBC or reading one of her books about money issues. "I don't know what they think they're going to live on," Applegarth says.

The idea of retirement as the pot of gold at the end of the rainbow is really not surprising, though, when you think about it. Americans simply want a piece of the good life they keep reading about.

Consider the cover story in the April 1997 issue of *Money* magazine. A young, single music teacher; a divorcing dad; a couple with young kids; another who own a business—all will retire with more than a million dollars and no sweat in getting there, according to this article. But read between the lines, and you'll see that the divorcing dad must invest the maximum $9,500 a year in his 403(b) retirement plan as well as "sock away" $2,400 *a month* in his stock portfolio to reach his goal. That's $28,800 after tax in addition to the $9,500 in the retirement plan. Wow! Few of us are doing that today. And few of us will be able to retire at age 50 or 55.

So instead of focusing on when you will drop the "ball-and-chain" and head for a sailboat in the Florida Keys, get real. Think about leaving your job as a transition and focus on what you really want to do when you switch gears. It's not just about money, either. If you've had a high-powered career and you've been going full-blast for 30 years, lying on the beach may look appealing. But it probably won't really appeal to the person you are. Adapting to a nonworking life requires considerable downshifting.

Take a look at Amy Saltzman's 1991 book by that name, which follows the careers of a number of ambitious professionals who elected to move off the fast track for personal reasons. They were people who took a step backwards professionally, who made a conscious decision to stay on a plateau, who shifted careers, who started their own businesses, or who escaped the big city for a rural life. But none of her subjects completely gave up working. They simply altered the terms of the employment agreement to suit them better. That's what you should be aiming for now.

When you think of what you want for yourself in the next stage of your life, think about these things:

◆ **Work.** What do you most want to do? How much money do you need to bring in from employment? If you really don't need any earned income, are there special projects that appeal to you? Charities? Family needs?

◆ **Location.** Another part of the American dream is to retire somewhere balmy. Do you want to relocate when you retire? What kind of lifestyle do you want? Do you love the city? The country? Another country? This is a big issue, and lots of people make mistakes because they don't give it the attention it deserves. If you're thinking of moving, experiment with your new lifestyle before you make an irrevocable decision.

◆ **Travel.** Isn't travel part of everyone's retirement plan? But what's really ideal for you? One big trip a year? Lots of long weekends? Camping? Spend some time mulling this over and planning what you most want to do.

◆ **Personal goals.** Do you want to take some courses? Learn French? Read Dostoyevsky? Take up gardening? Goals and achievement are critical parts of any stage of life.

PAY OFF DEBT

STEP 60

Americans at all stages of life carry too much debt—$475 billion in credit card debt alone in 1997, according to Federal Reserve Board figures. The average American pays $450 a year to carry a balance of $2,500 on two to three bankcards, says Ruth Susswein, executive director of BankCard Holders of America, a nonprofit group dedicated to helping consumers get out of debt.

As you prepare for retirement, paying off debt should be a top financial priority for two reasons. First, there's nowhere else you can get a guaranteed investment return equal to what you get by investing in your debt. Paying it off yields a risk-free return of whatever your interest rate happens to be. So paying off $2,500 at 16 percent yields a 16 percent return on that money. Second, it will give you flexibility by freeing up your cash flow.

Here's a plan to help you become debt-free:

1 Figure out how much you owe. Gather all your credit card statements and make a list that includes the interest rate, total balance, and minimum monthly payment. List the highest-rate card first and so on. "A lot of people have lost track of what they owe," says Gerri Detweiler, author of *The Ultimate Credit Handbook* (Plume/Penguin, 1997).

2 Keep the two cards with the lowest rates. Cut the others up. Write to the card issuers and ask that those accounts be closed.

3 If you do not have a card with an interest rate that is below 14 percent, get one. BankCard Holders of America offers a pamphlet, *Exactly how to get a low-interest rate credit card,* for $5. Write to BHA, 524 Branch Drive, Salem, VA 24153, for a copy.

4 Resolve that you will use your cards only for essentials over the next six months. For other purchases, use cash or a debit card. A debit card, which taps into your bank account when you make purchases, provides good discipline. If you don't have it, you can't spend it.

5 Add up your minimum monthly payments. Credit cards often require very low minimums. Follow them and you will be paying forever. For instance, if you owe $1,000 on a card with a 17 percent interest rate, Susswein says it might take you 12 years and cost you $979 to pay it off if you make only the minimum payment.

6 Calculate how much you can pay in addition to the minimum. Really stretch here. For instance, let's suppose the minimum payments on your credit cards total $350 a month. What could you pay if you really stretched? How about $750? No pain, no gain.

7 Apply all of your additional repayment to the card with the highest rate. If two cards have the same rate, put the additional money on the card with the largest balance. This makes the most effective use of your money because it saves you the most in interest.

8 Consolidate your debt. Many credit card issuers offer introductory rates as low as 5.9 percent or 6.9 percent for six months. If you are really serious about getting out of debt in a hurry, transfer your largest, high-rate balances to a card with an extremely low rate and pay them down *aggressively*. Monitor the rates carefully. When the rate goes up, shift to another card if you have not managed to pay off the balance.

9 Pay the minimum on your lowest-rate cards until you've paid off the balance on the more expensive cards.

10 Consider using your savings to get out of debt. Sure, it sounds harsh. But if you put together a balance sheet, your debt would cancel out your savings anyway. If those dollars are in the bank, you're earning around 2 percent to carry debt at 18 percent or more.

PAY DOWN THE MORTGAGE

STEP

61

Paying off credit card debt is a no-brainer. Although car loans generally carry lower interest rates than credit cards, they, too, should be paid off to prepare for the time when you will be living with a lower income. Interest on these loans is not tax deductible, so you carry the full cost of it. But paying off the mortgage is more controversial. Many investors argue they can get a better return on their money by investing in the stock market rather than in their own mortgage. Yet most financial planners advise clients to pay off their home before they retire.

Paying off the mortgage isn't a new idea. It has its roots in the debt aversion fostered in the Depression. It also has a modern missionary in Marc Eisenson, author of *The Banker's Secret (see Resources)*. In the book, Eisenson argues that by prepaying you are actually "investing in your mortgage," earning a return of whatever your interest rate happens to be.

Eisenson's book, which is composed chiefly of tables illustrating the effect of prepayments, shows, for example, that a homeowner who shells out an additional $200 a month shaves $153,414 in interest and more than six years off a $350,000, 30-year mortgage at 8 percent. The same $200 a month trims 11½ years off a $150,000 loan with similar terms.

Eisenson's case for prepayment is a powerful one. But savvy investors found it too simplistic. They argued that when you prepay a mortgage, you lose not only the tax deduction on the interest but also the opportunity to invest the funds elsewhere for a higher return. That made the idea workable only for those who didn't itemize or those in lower tax brackets. Those with big bucks—and big taxes—were better off with the deduction.

But a little-noticed tax change in 1990 reduced the dollar amount of most itemized deductions, including home mortgage interest, for those in the upper tax brackets. Beginning in 1991, taxpayers must subtract 3 percent of their adjusted gross income over $117,950 from their itemized deductions. "The mortgage interest deduction is clearly worth less to you now if you have a high income level," says Elaine Bedel, a financial planner in Indianapolis.

For these and other reasons, financial planners give serious thought to paying off the mortgage for clients at all stages of life. But for those nearing retirement, it's a slam-dunk, for psychological as well as economic reasons. Most people simply *feel* better knowing they own their home free and clear. "We don't make decisions for purely financial reasons," says Judith Shine, a planner in Englewood, Colorado. "We make decisions that help people live a happier life."

Shine, whose specialty is retirement and preretirement planning, says many of her clients are uncomfortable carrying debt, even though they have more than enough money to manage it. Peace of mind is far more important than leaving a large estate, she says. "I have never paid off a mortgage and had someone regret it," Shine says. "I've had people regret almost every other investment."

Of course, you can't expect to pay off a lump sum of $50,000 or $100,000 in one pop. But you can make investing in your mortgage something of a game. That's what Maureen McFadden, deputy editor at *Woman's Day,* is doing. McFadden weighs every purchase against paying extra on her mortgage, which she views as buying her freedom. That doesn't mean she sits home all the time. McFadden and her husband spent two weeks in Alaska in the summer of 1997, for instance. But they pay extra on their mortgage every month, too, so that, when they approach retirement age, they will have the freedom to travel as they like.

GATHER YOUR PAPERS

STEP 62 Being organized is important at all stages of your financial life. Still, most of us simply never get around to it and we still manage to muddle through. When you're heading for a big transition like retirement, though, order is essential.

Now you will need records that show how much you paid for your home and the cost of improvements you've made. You may need copies of your cash-value insurance policies, which can serve as a source of income in retirement. You'll need your birth certificate to apply for Social Security. And you must have pension records, investment records for stocks, bonds, and mutual funds, and records that show contributions and withdrawals from retirement accounts.

You also need to pull together some financial statements for your personal business. That means figuring out your net worth and then seeing what you might do to spruce it up a bit as well as an income statement or a budget that shows what's coming in and what's going out.

Start by pulling together these things:

◆ **A copy of your most recent income-tax return.**

◆ **Records of liquid assets.** You need to know exactly how much you have in checking and savings accounts, bank certificates of deposit, and money market accounts.

◆ **Copies of life insurance policies with records of accumulated cash values.** You should receive an annual statement from the insurer that shows current cash value as well as the current death benefit. On many policies, the death benefit increases as the policy generates what are called "paid up additions," or tiny little policies that are added to the big one. You'll want to know the current death benefit as well as your ability to generate tax-free income from your cash value. You can do this by taking tax-free loans from the policy, which need never be paid back provided you keep the policy in force. You need good advice on this strategy, so do some research to find it.

◆ **Annual statement from your employer that shows the value of your pension plan, 401(k) plan, and any other tax-deferred savings.**

◆ **A benefits statement that shows the value of life insurance and other employer benefits, as well as retiree medical benefits, if any.**

◆ **Statements for individual retirement accounts and Keogh plans for the self-employed.**

◆ **Records of investment assets including stocks, bonds, mutual funds, investment real estate, and limited partnerships.**

◆ **Information about real estate holdings.** If you own a home or apartment, figure out what you owe on your mortgage and what the home is worth. Ditto for a vacation home. Get information, too, on your car as well as a boat or motorcycle.

◆ **An estimate of the value of collectibles, including coins, antiques, art, or anything else of value.** Be realistic about the value of things like your comic book collection.

◆ **Records for valuable jewelry, furs, or Oriental rugs.** As a practical matter, your personal belongings like the clothes you wear to work and the couch in the living room don't add much to your net worth. But if you own some valuable stuff, you'll want to list it as an asset. Include here computer equipment.

◆ **Records of your debts including copies of a couple of recent credit card statements.** Also pull out payment books for your car and for any other personal loans, installment loans, or home-equity loans.

◆ **Records that show the value of your business, if you are self-employed.**

◆ **Records of business receivables.**

ORGANIZE YOUR RECORDS

STEP 63 Accountants say that people make two kinds of mistakes when it comes to keeping records. The first is to keep everything—expired refrigerator warranties, receipts from the donut shop, and last year's income tax return—in one jumbled box. The second is to throw everything out.

If you fall into either one of these groups, there's hope for you. Like most other financial tasks, record keeping is not difficult. At the beginning it may be time consuming, but once you get your files set up, maintenance is fairly simple.

Make six file folders:

◆ **Personal,** which includes all family records, such as birth and marriage papers, adoption and custody papers, university diplomas, military papers, membership certificates, licenses, wills;

◆ **Property,** which includes documents like deeds, receipts, and appraisals;

◆ **Financial,** which includes investments, IRAs, 401(k) accounts, loan papers, credit card records, bank accounts, trust agreements, mutual fund statements;

◆ **Insurance,** for your policies and claim settlement records and receipts;

◆ **Tax;**

◆ **Medical,** for health records and prescriptions, statements from hospitals, reports of medical exams.

Here are some rules of thumb on what to keep:

Personal records that document birth, marriage, and divorce should be kept forever. Other records that should be kept indefinitely include military papers, medical records, and wills and trust agreements.

Include, too, in your "keep forever" files brokerage and mutual fund statements, stock option agreements, and other investment papers. Records on property you inherit should also be kept. Your "cost basis," or the cost on which your capital gains tax will be calculated, is determined by the property's market value when you inherited it. People without records may be forced to pay capital gains on the entire sales price.

You should also keep retirement plan agreements, insurance policies, wills, trust agreements, and powers of attorney.

The Internal Revenue Service has three years from the time of filing to assess additional taxes. For that reason, many people believe they need to keep tax records for only three years. But the statue of limitations stretches to six years if a taxpayer omits income exceeding 25 percent of the income reported. And there is no statute of limitations on returns where the IRS finds fraud. Keeping tax records for 10 years—or even longer—makes sense.

Keep with your tax records those records of property that has a "cost basis" for tax purposes. These include records that document what you paid for your home and money you laid out for improvements. These records must be kept until you sell the property so that you can establish your basis for capital gains purposes.

Consumer records such as receipts, invoices, and warranties need be kept only as long as you own the property. While you're getting organized, though, make a list of credit cards with their phone numbers so that you can call the company in the event they are stolen. List, too, your financial representatives, including your accountant, insurance agent, financial planner, or stockbroker—and their phone numbers. Keep this list with your financial records.

CALCULATE YOUR NET WORTH

STEP

64

You need a balance sheet to show what you own and what you owe as well as the decisions you've made about spending your money over the years. It should be divided into two broad categories: assets, or what you have, and liabilities, or what you owe. The assets category is subdivided into three smaller categories: liquid, investment, and personal assets.

A liquid asset like a bank checking account has an indisputable cash value. Personal assets—clothes, furnishings, electronics—are often called "wasting assets" because they begin to decrease in value as soon as you buy them. Keep in mind that you will not be able to resell them for what you paid. A one-of-a-kind Oriental rug can be listed at the price you paid. But a television set or computer should probably be listed at half what you paid.

NET WORTH STATEMENT

◆ Liquid assets

Cash (checking, savings accounts)	$ _____
Certificates of deposit	_____
Money market funds	_____
Other	_____
Total liquid assets	**$ _____**

◆ Investment assets

Stock	$ _____
Bonds	_____
Mutual funds	_____
Life-insurance cash values	_____
Investment real estate	_____
Limited partnerships	_____
Collectibles	_____
Precious metals	_____
Other	_____
Total investment assets	**$ _____**

◆ **Personal assets**

Personal residence	$ _____
Vacation home	_____
Automobiles	_____
Household furnishings/rugs	_____
Clothing/jewelry	_____
Computer equipment	_____
Total personal assets	$ _____
TOTAL ASSETS	$ _____

Now list everything you owe:

◆ **Short-term debt**

MasterCard/Visa	$ _____
Bank overdraft line	_____
Home equity loans	_____
Student/business loans	_____
Total short-term debt	$ _____

◆ **Long-term debt**

Home mortgage	$ _____
Mortgage on second home	_____
Total long-term debt	$ _____
TOTAL DEBT	$ _____

Now subtract your liabilities—or debt—from your assets. That's your net worth. Look at how your wealth is spread among the three asset classes. To be prepared for emergencies, you need three months' worth of living expenses in liquid assets. To accomplish your future goals, you need investments. They are the engine for the growth of your balance sheet. Once you have set aside your emergency fund, pump as much as possible into investments.

If your balance sheet shows that most of your assets are in the personal category, think about changing the way you deploy your money. You should aim to increase your net worth each year—by paying down debt and pumping more money into your 401(k) and other investments.

DRAW UP A
FINANCIAL STATEMENT

STEP

65

To figure out what you'll need in retirement, you need to know how much you earn now and how much of it you spend. That means you need a monthly financial statement or a budget. To come up with one, write down everything you spend for a month. That includes your mortgage payment, car payment, utilities, food, etc. Then spend a few hours going through your checkbook and credit card bills to find those things you missed, like life insurance premiums, vacations, Christmas gifts.

Expenses come in two categories—fixed and discretionary—but some items fall in both camps: clothing, for instance, and food. There are the basics, like underwear and orange juice, and there are the luxuries, like a cashmere sweater and caviar.

List your sources of income, then split your expenses into fixed and discretionary and list them here.

MONTHLY INCOME

Salary from job	$ _____
Receipts from business, consulting	_____
Investment income	_____
Rental income	_____
TOTAL MONTHLY INCOME	$ _____

FIXED EXPENSES

Federal/state taxes	$ _____
Social Security taxes	_____
401(k) contribution	_____
Savings	_____
Mortgage payment	_____
Property tax	_____
Utilities	_____
Homeowner's insurance	_____
Telephone	_____

Rent   _____
Renter's insurance   _____
Groceries   _____
Clothing   _____
Transportation:
—Car payments   _____
—Car insurance   _____
—Gas/maintenance   _____
—Bus, train, or subway fare   _____
Life insurance   _____
Disability insurance   _____
Health insurance   _____
Credit card repayments   _____
Personal care (haircuts, dry cleaning, etc.) _____
  Total fixed expenses $ _____

DISCRETIONARY EXPENSES

Meals out $ _____
Movies, video rentals   _____
Cab fare and rental cars   _____
Housecleaning help   _____
Facials, manicures, massage   _____
Entertaining   _____
Clothing   _____
Jewelry   _____
Sports equipment   _____
Vacations   _____
Health club   _____
Charitable contributions   _____
Books, magazines   _____
Gifts   _____
  Total discretionary expenses $ _____
      TOTAL MONTHLY EXPENSES $ _____

Look at your fixed expenses. It is this amount that you must
cover both now and in retirement.

REVIEW YOUR PORTFOLIO

STEP

66

Reviewing and repositioning your investment portfolio for retirement is a key part of preparing for transition. You have saved throughout your working years. Now you must take stock and see if you have what you need to last the remainder of your lifetime and, if not, what you might do about it.

When you think about your investment portfolio, think about *all* your assets. That includes your personal residence, a second home if you have one, a family business, the money in all your retirement plans, and the assets you have outside your retirement accounts. Look at the balance sheet you've just prepared as a start.

Your balance sheet provides a list of your assets. But you want to see what your portfolio looks like—or how those assets are grouped by investment category. *(For more detailed advice on how to set up an investment portfolio, see Part 8, "Sample Portfolios.")*

Roger Gibson, an investment manager who is author of *Asset Allocation: Balancing Financial Risk*, (Dow Jones-Irwin, 1990), suggests that you divide your assets into two broad categories. The first is those that produce income such as bonds, money market funds, and Treasury bills. Include here any benefit that you will receive from a traditional pension plan or defined benefit plan. That represents a fixed income because the monthly benefit is fixed.

The second is investments that represent ownership or equity. That includes stocks. It also includes real estate that you own directly, whether it is your residence or vacation home or investment property. And it includes other ownership investments like a family business if you have one.

How do you decide how to allocate these assets? William G. Droms, a professor of finance at Georgetown University and a popular speaker on this topic, devised a shorthand method. Value the seven statements on a scale of 1 to 5, with 1 being "strongly disagree" and 5 being "strongly agree." Then add up your points.

◆ Earning a high long-term total return that will allow my capital to grow faster than the inflation rate is one of my most important investment objectives.

◆ I would like an investment that provides me with an opportunity to defer taxation of capital gains and/or interest to future years.

◆ I do not require a high level of current income from my investments.

◆ My major investment goals are relatively long term.

◆ I am willing to tolerate sharp up-and-down swings in the return on my investments in order to seek a higher return than would be expected from more stable investments.

◆ I am willing to risk a short-term loss in return for a potentially higher rate of return in the long run.

◆ I am financially able to accept a low level of liquidity in my investment portfolio.

Depending on how you scored, here are Droms's recommendations on what percentage of assets to put into each sort of investment:

TOTAL SCORE	MONEY MARKET	FIXED INCOME	EQUITIES
30 to 35	10	10	80
22 to 29	20	20	60
14 to 21	30	30	40
7 to 13	40	40	20

Financial planners like Droms's test because it acknowledges the different tugs and pulls on investments and comes up with a neat score to determine asset allocation. "It's the best test I've seen," says Harold Evensky, who designed our sample portfolios in Part 8.

DON'T MOVE OUT OF STOCKS

STEP 67
Traditional advice to retirees was this: Sell your stocks. Buy bonds. Stocks are for young, aggressive investors who have time to let their money grow and who can ride out the bumps. As a retiree, you need the smoother ride provided by bonds, as well as the income. You no longer need growth. You are in a phase of your life when you can safely consume assets.

Times have changed. Over the past decade bonds have become nearly as volatile as stocks. But they still hold less return potential than stocks—a good 2 percent less on average, according to Sanford C. Bernstein & Co., a Wall Street research house. Retirees need that extra return because most don't have much flexibility in terms of generating earned income. Inflation risk looms large when earned income stops. And life expectancies have increased so much that retirees cannot safely begin consuming assets when they first retire.

If a couple retires at age 65 in average health, at least one of the spouses can expect to live 20 years or more, says Roger Gibson, an investment manager who is author of *Asset Allocation: Balancing Financial Risk,* (Dow Jones-Irwin Inc., 1990). "Now is not the time to put your portfolio to sleep," Gibson says.

If you can leave a good chunk of your money in stocks, you'll have more money to live on in retirement. Money that you will not need for living expenses for five years or more is a good candidate for the stock market. "Our clients who are in their sixties are still 60 percent invested in stocks," says H. Lynn Hopewell, a financial planner in Falls Church, Virginia. Gibson, too, recommends that the majority of your money be in stocks, but adds that the stocks should be globally diversified.

If you need to receive income from the money you've accumulated, you must move a portion of it into income-paying securities. But they need not be bond funds. You could choose a diversified income fund like Spectrum Income, which invests in a variety of foreign and domestic bond funds and an equity income fund. Or you might put a portion into an equity income fund itself, which invests in stocks that pay high dividends, preferred stocks, utilities, and REITs in an effort to pay out a steady income.

Equity income funds are one of the best-performing groups of stock funds. In addition to growth and income, most offer a steady, stable performance without a great deal of volatility. T. Rowe Price, Fidelity, and Vanguard all have consistent performers in this category. Other candidates for growth with an income kicker are hybrid funds like Lindner Dividend and balanced funds like Dodge and Cox Balanced.

Sheldon Jacobs, editor of *The No-Load Fund Investor*, an investment newsletter based in Irvington-on-Hudson, New York, compiles suggested portfolios of no-load funds for investors at different stages of life. His portfolios for retirees contain a healthy dose of stocks, though they are a bit more conservative than the portfolios for workers.

Here are some types of funds that retirees might consider:

◆ **Index funds,** which invest in the broad market, as measured by the Standard & Poor's Index of 500 stocks. The best of these is the Vanguard Index 500 Trust.

◆ **Conservative international funds** like T. Rowe Price International Stock or SoGen International.

◆ **Consistent value funds** like the Mutual Series funds, Dodge & Cox Stock, and Longleaf Partners.

◆ **Funds of funds,** which combine a number of mutual funds under one roof, like Vanguard STAR, or Spectrum Growth.

◆ **Solid balanced funds** like Vanguard/Wellington.

LOOK AT TAXES
BEFORE YOU MOVE

STEP

68

For many Americans, heading south in retirement is part of a lifetime dream. That was true for Stanley and Phyllis Kempner, who left New Jersey and retired to a large home with a pool in Hollywood, Florida, when Kempner sold his printing business. Although the Kempners have been happy in Florida, they don't believe they've found paradise. "I don't want you to have the idea this is utopia down here," Kempner says. "We have the same problems as anywhere else. It's just that we have the weather to mitigate it."

For instance, Florida has no income tax and housing costs are lower. But medical costs are high in Florida. And the state does have a 6 percent sales tax as well as a 1.5 percent tax on intangibles, such as financial property. Costs also vary widely in different parts of the same state. So it pays to check carefully before you make a move. It's important, too, to establish your residence in your new state so that you don't get stuck paying taxes—and estate taxes—in both states.

Until recently, many northern states attempted to levy a tax on retirees who moved to another state. But Congress passed a law in 1996 outlawing that practice. Still, if you plan to move you should pay attention to the way states tax pension and retirement income. Many taxpayers overlook the state rules because at the federal level, taxes are levied on retirement withdrawals.

Some northern states have made moves recently to appeal to retirees, too. For example, in 1997 New York state passed a law that will gradually eliminate that state's high estate tax. Thanks largely to the efforts of Joshua Rubenstein, a trusts and estates lawyer at Rosenman & Colin in New York, the state decided to roll back the estate tax to make New York competitive with states such as Florida that were attracting affluent New York retirees. In a few years, a New Yorker will pay no extra estate tax if he lives in New York. Because New York is a leader in tax law changes, other states are certain to look at these types of changes. So before you flee to the South, be certain that your information about taxes is based on fact, not rumor or history.

Still, states have some quirky rules that might catch you up short in retirement. For example, in Louisiana, residents who take their pension money as a lump sum pay no state tax. But those who elect regular payments over their lifetimes pay up to 6 percent in state taxes. If the taxpayer with the lump sum rolls it into an IRA, all of it becomes taxable on the state level.

New York residents can take $20,000 a year in retirement income from pensions and other sources free of state tax. But amounts over that are taxed. If pension money is distributed as a lump sum or rolled over to an IRA, it is taxable in New York. But it can escape the tax if it is distributed as an annuity.

Some states, like Pennsylvania, do not permit a tax deduction for money going into retirement accounts like 401(k)s or IRAs. But they do not tax withdrawals either. New Jersey does not permit a tax deduction for money going into the account and the amount contributed can be withdrawn free of tax. But the earnings are taxed at withdrawal.

In some cases, a taxpayer can profit by moving. Suppose a taxpayer who spends his working life in Delaware, which grants a tax deduction for retirement accounts and does not levy tax on withdrawals by former residents, moves to Pennsylvania or Florida, which do not tax withdrawals. That person pays no state taxes at all.

When researching taxes, don't forget to look at property taxes and other types of levies as well. Don't rely on word of mouth that taxes are "insignificant."

DELAY COLLECTING SOCIAL SECURITY IF YOU CAN

STEP

69

One of the most commonly asked questions about Social Security benefits is this: Should I wait until age 65 or should I take a reduced benefit at age 62?

Workers who were born in 1937 or before earn full benefits at age 65. If they decide to receive benefits at age 62, the earliest permissible age to receive benefits, those benefits are reduced by 20 percent. That reduction is *permanent*. So if your earned benefit is $1,000 and you begin collecting your $800 at age 62, the $800, plus cost of living adjustments, is what you will receive for the rest of your life.

There are a number of sophisticated arguments put forward that compare the appeal of early, reduced benefits to later, full benefits. They rely on life expectancy and the expected rate of return. For example, if you are able to get a 12 percent return on your reduced benefit, you will come out ahead. Likewise, if you live only until age 66, you will come out ahead with the reduced benefit. However, the reduced benefit is designed to be an "actuarial equivalent." What that means is that on average workers come out the same financially under each alternative.

But you want to know how you will fare, not how the average person fares. Dale R. Detlefs probably knows more about the ins and outs of the Social Security system than just about anybody else in the country. He's definitely in the top five, knowledgewise. For 20 years, he was manager of the Social Security division of William M. Mercer, Inc., the world's largest benefits consulting firm. Each year he coauthors a guide to Social Security and Medicare for Mercer. In 1992, at age 65, Detlefs cut back to half-time with Mercer, although he still managed the Social Security division. A couple of years later, he cut back again, this time to a consulting role.

So in the spring of 1997, when I wanted to provide advice on when people should begin collecting Social Security benefits, I gave Detlefs a call. Detlefs, who is 70, and his wife had just returned from a five-week cruise on the *Queen Elizabeth II*. When did he begin receiving Social Security benefits? I asked. At age 70. At that point, there is no longer any penalty for earning income. In other words, no matter how much you earn, your benefits are not reduced. And after age 70, you no longer earn extra credits for delaying retirement. Up until age 70, your benefit is increased if you delay receiving it. So Detlefs receives the maximum possible benefit. So should you if you can possibly swing it.

There are some additional rules that are important here. For example, Social Security payments are taxable for many recipients. Some must pay income tax on 50 percent of their benefits; others must pay tax on 85 percent. Working reduces benefits, too *(see* **STEP 70***)*. And the normal retirement age is edging up. It increases gradually so that those born after 1959 are not eligible for 100 percent of their benefit until age 67. If they choose to receive benefits at age 62, they will get just 70 percent of their earned benefit.

Finally, the law awards delayed retirement credits for those who work beyond the normal retirement age of 65. These delayed retirement credits can be earned up to age 70. Those who reach their normal retirement age in 1997, but delay receiving benefits, will earn a 5 percent increase in benefits for each year they delay. That delayed retirement credit increases one-half of 1 percent each year until it reaches 8 percent for those born in 1943, which is an actuarial equivalent. That means you will be "paid" a fair amount to continue working and to delay receiving your benefit until age 70. The younger you are, the more changes you should expect along these lines.

CONSIDER WHETHER
YOU WILL WORK

STEP
70

When you are planning your retirement, think carefully about whether you will earn any employment income. If you work, you are likely to give up Social Security benefits—and you may be taxed on those benefits you do receive. In some cases, working actually reduces your after-tax income, thanks to a 1993 change in the tax law that taxes up to 85 percent of Social Security benefits.

It's easy to brush this off as a disincentive to working in retirement. And it is. But it's also a disincentive to apply early for Social Security. If you know that you will work and earn income, think carefully about whether you might be better off delaying Social Security benefits and picking up the delayed retirement credit for doing so.

There are two layers of taxes and lost benefits to consider. First is the retirement earnings limitation. This defines what you can earn in retirement before you begin losing benefits. Those retirees aged 62 through 64 give up $1 in Social Security benefits for each $2 they earn over $8,640 in 1997. Those aged 65 to 69 give up $1 in Social Security benefits for each $3 they earn over $13,500 in 1997. That limit increases to $14,500 in 1998, $15,500 in 1999, $17,000 in 2000, $25,000 in 2001, and $30,000 in 2002. There is no earnings limitation for those age 70 and older.

In their 1997 *Mercer Guide to Social Security & Medicare*, which is the most authoritative guide on this subject, Dale Detlefs and Robert J. Myers give this example: Suppose you are 65 and begin receiving Social Security retirement benefits in 1997. You earn $43,500, which is $30,000 more than the permissible amount of $13,500. The loss in benefits is $10,000— or one in three dollars of the excess.

Detlefs and Myers also explain that you may use a monthly test instead in the first year when you are entitled to benefits if it gives you better results. During that first year, you are entitled to your monthly benefit if you do not earn more than one-twelfth of the earnings limitation—or $1,125. If you earn more than one-twelfth of the annual limit, you revert to the annual test.

The earnings limitation reduces benefits. And the 1993 tax law taxes up to 85 percent of those benefits you do receive. Beginning in 1994, couples with more than $44,000 in income and singles with more than $34,000 pay tax on 85 percent of their benefits. In some cases, working retirees actually lose money by working.

The impact is greatest on retirees whose work pushes their incomes slightly above those limits. "The absolute worst effect comes where the loss of benefits overlaps with the taxation of 85 percent of benefits," says Kjeld Sorensen, a lawyer and accountant in the research center of the Wyatt Company, a benefits consulting company based in Washington, D.C. "The first factor reduces your Social Security. The second factor results in an add-back, where you are paying taxes on 85 percent of the Social Security benefit."

For example, Sorensen worked out an example where a single retiree earned $2,000 above the income limit and was forced to give back $1,000 in benefits. But the taxable income of this retiree rose by $3,275. "Your cash inflow may go up by $1,000, but your taxable income would rise by $3,275 because the amount of taxable wages grew and the amount of benefits you had to pay taxes on grew," he says. After federal tax, this single taxpayer would lose $70 for earning the additional $2,000, Sorensen says.

If you plan to work and your income would result in lost benefits and higher taxes, consider the alternative: delaying Social Security to receive a higher benefit.

CONSIDER LONG-TERM-CARE INSURANCE

STEP
71

A decade ago, Peter J. Strauss, a prominent New York elder care attorney, would not recommend long-term-care policies to his clients. In fact, so worthless were the available policies in Strauss's estimation that he preferred to help well-off clients do something that many people consider shameful: Qualify for Medicaid, which means going into a nursing home at government expense, while still protecting some personal assets.

Strauss was certainly not alone. Indeed, the Medicaid program ballooned along with the number of people—both rich and poor—who turned their nursing home bills over to the government. Medicaid now pays for half of all long-term-care expenses. That fact did not go unnoticed by policy makers, who began looking for ways to get those who could afford to do so to contribute to their own long-term-care needs. The best way to do that, of course, was to improve the insurance policies and to persuade more people to buy them.

Over the past seven or eight years, the policies have been improved. So much so that Deena Katz, a financial planner in Coral Gables, Florida, who specializes in long-term care, thinks they are as good as they're going to get. "They've tweaked them six ways from Sunday," Katz says. "There's no reason now not to buy one." In fact, there are lots of reasons *to* buy one.

The argument for buying a policy is this: Americans at age 65 have a 43 percent chance of needing long-term care, according to David E. Hughes, senior vice president for long-term care at UNUM, a major insurer in this market based in Portland, Maine. The earlier you buy the policy the better, because you lock in a level premium for life. "You can't afford to wait,"

Strauss says. "It's a wonderful buy at 55. It's still a relatively good buy at 60. At age 65 and up, it starts to get expensive." Further, as you age you may develop health problems that will make you uninsurable. For example, Katz says, "I'm 47 and I won't be able to buy it because I have chronic back disease." Ditto with arthritis and other problems of aging.

At the same time, it has become extremely difficult to qualify for Medicaid unless you are truly destitute. On January 1, 1997, as part of the Health Insurance Portability and Accountability Act, it became a crime to transfer assets in order to qualify for Medicaid nursing home benefits, although a later clarification of that law put the responsibility on the financial adviser rather than the Medicaid applicant.

The same law offered a carrot by making long-term-care premiums tax-deductible and making benefits tax free, provided the insurer writes policies that qualify for this tax break. All the big reputable companies do, Katz says. When you're shopping, be sure you ask that question.

The problem with the early policies was that they put too many limits on the payment of benefits. For example, most tied payment of benefits to some medical condition and might require a hospital stay before a policyholder could qualify. What has been recognized over the years is that most long-term-care is simply custodial—the old and frail need someone to help them with the activities of daily living like eating and bathing.

The best policies offer a great deal of flexibility and allow you to use your benefits as you wish. They work something like prefunding a bank account today that you will be able to draw on when you need it. For example, if you buy a policy with a maximum benefit of $100 a day for three years, that amounts to a lifetime benefit of $109,500. If you use a home health aide at $50 a day for one year, you would have a balance of $91,250.

PUT HEALTH CARE IN PLACE

STEP

72

Time was when corporations paid not just retirement benefits but health care benefits as well to their retirees. Those expensive benefits all but disappeared. More than 70 percent of large employers cut back on retiree health care in the mid 1990s, according to the annual health care survey by Foster Higgins, a benefits consulting firm.

Employers made changes for two reasons: because health care costs were rising rapidly and because the Financial Accounting Standards Board required large companies to begin carrying future retiree health costs as a liability on their books in 1993. That means retirees of all ages must think about their own health care. But the problem is especially acute for those who retire before age 65 because that is the age when benefits begin through the government-run Medicare program. So if you are contemplating early retirement you will want to begin by examining your company's medical provisions for retirees, remembering that there is no guarantee that the plan will remain intact.

Understanding what your company is likely to do may help in planning. Some companies ask retirees to contribute more to insurance premiums. Others increase deductibles and coinsurance amounts, which are payments made directly by retirees. Others might set a cutoff point such as no retiree medical for employees hired after a certain date, or no medical care in retirement for anyone who is still an active employee today. Or they eliminate it for those under a certain age or perhaps for those who are more than five years away from retirement. Some companies have actually eliminated paid health care for those who have already retired. Others—like AT&T, CBS, Control Data, Goodyear, and Kmart—put caps on their retiree coverage, according to Jerry Y. Carnegie, a principal in the Rowayton, Connecticut, office of Hewitt Associates, benefits consultants. A cap might work like this: when the average retiree medical cost reaches 1.5 or 2 times its current level, the company will pass on additional costs to the individual. The cap allows companies to control the charges that could depress earnings.

Long before you retire, you should check your company's benefits. Some companies are making changes that mean employees must earn retiree health care benefits in much the same way that they earn pension benefits. In that case, you might have to work for your employer for a set number of years before you are entitled to retiree health care. Find out what your employer promises to give you, how many years you have to work to get those benefits, and how easy or hard it is for your employer to change them. If you are married, review your spouse's coverage, too. If one spouse plans to retire while the other works, the retiree might be covered through the other's medical plan.

No matter how generous or stingy your employer is, you will have some benefits under the Consolidated Omnibus Budget Reconciliation Act of 1986, or Cobra. This law allows an employee to continue group health insurance coverage for 18 months after leaving the company for the cost of coverage plus a 2 percent fee. The Cobra coverage may seem expensive, but as a group plan, it will almost certainly be less costly than buying an individual policy.

Once those benefits are exhausted, companies with insured plans must allow people to convert from the group plan to an individual plan. This coverage tends to be very limited, but a medical exam is not required. Another possibility is a group plan through a professional association, fraternal society, or the American Association of Retired Persons.

Medical coverage is critical. Examine your options carefully and make health insurance a key part of transition planning.

PART

6

STEPS
To Take in
Retirement

ISIT ANY NEWSSTAND and you're likely to see a half dozen magazine cover stories on retirement: How to save a million dollars; how to retire at 50. There's no shortage of advice on how to save money, how much you should save, and where to invest it. This is the glamorous stuff of planning for retirement. Unfortunately, good advice on how to pull all that money out of retirement accounts when you need it is as scarce as hen's teeth. Yet good advice in this area could make a difference of thousands —or even hundreds of thousands of dollars.

When I was writing a personal finance column for *The New York Times,* there was only one source I considered fail-safe on this issue: Seymour Goldberg, a lawyer and an expert on plan distributions in Garden City, New York. But whenever I wrote a column detailing Goldberg's strategies, I always received letters from readers who said their own financial advisers told them that these techniques were not permissible. Then I would check with the Internal Revenue Service and find that, indeed, Goldberg was correct and it was the other advisers who were wrong. Since then, a number of financial planners, like Jim Budros in Columbus, Ohio, have developed specialties in this area. Still, you can't count on finding one of them when you're ready to take your money out.

Making a mistake in this area can be extremely costly. If you have a great deal of money in your plan, I suggest that you get one of Goldberg's books, which are listed in the resource list, or even that you hire him for a consultation. You cannot afford errors here.

DON'T TAKE THE
MONEY AND RUN

STEP

73

When you retire with a lump sum of money in your 401(k) plan, it belongs to you. Whether it is $20,000 or $1.2 million, you are entitled to take it home with you. If you take it out of your 401(k) and deposit it in the bank, though, you will owe taxes on all of it. Remember when we talked about the government's role in 401(k) plans? This is where the government gets the payoff for all those years of tax deferral. So if you took a lump sum of $1 million, roughly one third to one half of that would go to taxes.

One option you might have, provided you were born before January 1, 1936, is to use 10-year forward averaging. This favorable method of paying tax is being phased out and is available only to those who were born before 1936. However, it allows those eligible taxpayers to pay tax as if the money from their qualified plan is the only money they received over a 10-year period. So your $1 million would be taxed as if you received $100,000 each year for 10 years.

Because this method uses tax rates that were in effect in 1986, the formula for figuring taxes on this method is complicated. But if you are at least 59½, have been a participant in your plan for at least five calendar years, and were born before 1936, you should have an accountant figure out the tax implications of using this method.

Some taxpayers will want to consider leaving the money with their employer *(see* **STEP 74***)*. But most taxpayers will probably want to roll their 401(k) money into an individual retirement account. This preserves its tax-deferred status until you begin making mandatory withdrawals from the account at age 70½.

One big advantage to an IRA is that the money is no longer off limits to you. Provided that you are over

59½, you can tap into the money whenever you like, paying tax on it as you withdraw it. For many Americans, the chunk of money from their retirement plan represents the biggest asset they have. If you are one of them and you have little investing experience, either do some research or get help.

Investing the money yourself is possible. You need three things. First, an asset allocation model. That's a plan for how you will split your money between different types of investments like stocks, bonds, and cash. Second, you need either individual securities or mutual funds to build your portfolio. And third, you need the discipline to sit tight through thick and thin. The best way to fritter away your life savings is by tinkering with your investment mix every time you read a newspaper or magazine story. If you plan to do it on your own, read Part 8, "Sample Portfolios," carefully, which describes allocations devised by Harold Evensky, an investment manager in Coral Gables, Florida. You also might find Sheldon Jacobs's *No-Load Fund Investor* to be of value. Jacobs sets up asset allocations using no-load mutual funds.

Some good financial planners are willing to set up an asset allocation for a flat fee. Bob Wacker, a planner in San Luis Obispo, California, comes to mind. Wacker says he will do an investment review and make investment recommendations for as little as $750. That does not include any investment monitoring. If you are going to use a portfolio allocation from a planner like Wacker—or from Sheldon Jacobs's newsletter— you must not get cold feet when the markets plunge. If you believe that you cannot hang on on your own, go straight to a financial planner and have the money invested. Do not try to do it on your own. Hand-holding from a financial planner can be expensive. It can also be priceless. If you get emotional about your money, high-priced help is worth every penny.

CONSIDER LEAVING MONEY
WITH YOUR EMPLOYER

STEP

74

Most employees take their 401(k) money with them when they retire. But it's not always the wisest move. There are some compelling reasons to leave your retirement money with your employer. For instance, you may have special investment options that you can't duplicate outside the plan. Or your employer may subsidize the plan in some way.

Qualified plans—which include the 401(k)—sometimes have legal advantages over individual retirement accounts, too. For example, the money in a qualified plan cannot be tapped by your creditors if you declare bankruptcy. (It's also safe in the event of your company's bankruptcy.) But IRA money typically can. Money in qualified plans is also eligible for more favorable tax treatments, such as forward averaging. When Congress makes new rules about retirement plans, they usually apply to qualified ones, but not to IRAs.

So you shouldn't *automatically* decide to take the money with you. Do some checking first. Find out what happens if you leave it in the plan. The basic guideline is this: If you have $3,500 or less in your 401(k), your employer is permitted to write you a check to cash you out of the plan and end the administrative fees associated with your account. If you have more than $3,500, your employer *must* permit you to remain in the plan.

What you should be interested in is your employer's attitude toward you and your 401(k) money. As you know by now, employers used 401(k) plans to shift the responsibility for retirement investing to employees. Some are eager to be done with it. They really don't want you in the plan for any longer than necessary. Look for signs of this attitude in the

401(k) materials your employer furnishes. Other employers want retirees to stay to help pay the bills. Retirees require fewer services than active employees, yet they have higher account balances. So if the plan fees are based on a percent of assets, the retirees subsidize the active employees.

Another group of employers feels very responsible for employees' retirement goals. This group may provide special enticements to keep employees in the plan so that the company knows their money is protected in retirement. Consider, for example, what Albany International Corporation, a supplier to the paper industry based in Albany, New York, did to assist its employees. Beginning in 1994, the company permitted employees to put all or part of their 401(k) balance into the company pension plan and receive it in monthly payouts as a supplement to regular pension income. That allows employees to get professional money management by a pension expert and a steady stream of income.

The monthly payout plan resembles an annuity purchased from an insurance company—with a couple of important differences. Unlike an insurer, Albany International offers the plan at no cost to employees. Buying an annuity with similar features would be expensive, says Hanora Sarro, a consultant with William M. Mercer Inc., the benefits consultants who designed the plan. Mercer surveyed the annuity market to see how the plan stacked up. Albany International's return was about *18 percent* better than the best annuity they could find because there was no sales commission and no fees attached to the company's plan.

When you get close to retirement, schedule an interview with your human resources department. Talk, too, with recent retirees and try to get a sense of how the company treats them in the plan before you make your decision. Look carefully, too, at the plan's expenses.

CONSIDER CONVERTING
TO A ROTH IRA

STEP

75

One of the most interesting provisions of the new Roth IRA introduced by the Taxpayer Relief Act of 1997 is the ability of taxpayers with adjusted gross income of less than $100,000 to convert from a traditional deductible or nondeductible IRA to the new Roth. All the money that is converted is taxable provided it has not yet been taxed. But it does not carry the 10 percent penalty for early withdrawal. If the conversion is completed in 1998, the tax due can be paid over a four-year period.

Those who are retiring with large balances in their qualified plans, such as 401(k) plans and other pensions, should look at the pros and cons of converting this money to the Roth IRA. That can be done by rolling it into a traditional IRA and then paying the tax and converting. Steven Norwitz, a vice president at T. Rowe Price & Associates, the Baltimore-based mutual fund company, spent much of the second half of 1997 working on comparisons of the cash flow a retiree would receive if he used the Roth IRA compared to the traditional deductible IRA. "The Roth IRA wins almost every time," Norwitz says.

Although there is no tax deduction for money contributed to a Roth, withdrawals from the account are completely tax free. Furthermore, there is no mandatory withdrawal schedule. You don't even need to take the money out during your lifetime. You can continue to contribute to the account as long as you earn employment income. With the traditional IRA, you cannot contribute after age 70½. And the money from a Roth IRA is not included in taxable income when you withdraw it, which can make a difference in calculating the taxability of your Social Security income.

All these factors certainly make the new Roth IRA attractive. But it is the ability to let the money continue to grow tax deferred that represents the biggest advantage. Clearly, the more time you have, the bigger the advantage. But Norwitz says he calculated the benefit for a 65-year-old and found that he would be better off by converting to the Roth IRA even if he started withdrawing the money five years later. Norwitz's calculations assume that you have the money elsewhere to pay the tax. If you must pay the tax out of the money in the IRA account, it doesn't make sense to convert, Norwitz says.

If you do have the money elsewhere, you should consider converting even if you're close to the time when you will use the money. "Let's say you have $1 million in a plan and you are nearing age 70½," says Gregory Kolojeski, a tax attorney. "Your tax deferral is about to end," because of mandatory withdrawals. But if you convert to a Roth IRA, "you are adding a generation or at least several decades of deferral. People who would be running out of tax deferral are ahead of the game in just a handful of years," says Kolojeski, who is working on software to compare the Roth and traditional IRAs for Brentmark Software, his company based in Winter Park, Florida.

Paying tax on all your retirement savings and converting to the Roth IRA represents a big decision. If you convert before December 31, 1998, you are permitted to stretch the tax payments over four years. Take your time. Get some help. There will be a lot of discussion on this issue during 1998. One good place to find the latest information is on Kolojeski's new Web site (rothira.com). Get a copy, too, of the T. Rowe Price IRA Analyzer (800-333-0740), which helps you compare the Roth IRA and a traditional IRA.

LOOK AT THE
DISTRIBUTION OPTIONS

STEP

76

You must begin taking money from tax-deferred retirement accounts—which include individual retirement accounts and 401(k) plans—by April 1 of the year following the calendar year in which you turn 70½ unless you are still working. If you are a participant in a qualified plan, like a 401(k), and you are still working, you may postpone withdrawals under the terms of a 1996 law.

For those who must begin withdrawals, there are two methods permitted, according to Seymour Goldberg, a tax attorney in Garden City, New York, and one of the leading experts in this arcane area. The first, the "recalculation method," is used by most taxpayers merely because they are unaware of the other option.

With the recalculation method, a taxpayer turning 70½ in 1997 calculates a minimum withdrawal based on personal life expectancy as determined by actuarial tables or the joint life expectancy of himself and his beneficiary. Each year the distribution is recalculated. (Life expectancies in actuarial tables decrease each year, but not by a full year. For example, a 70-year-old husband and his 67-year-old wife have a joint life expectancy of 22 years. A year later, their life expectancy would be 21.2 years.)

Suppose this couple selected the recalculation method. If the man turned 70½ in 1997, they must determine the retirement account balance as of December 31, 1996 and withdraw 1/22 of that amount by April 1, 1998. The next year, they would recalculate the balance as of December 31, 1997, and withdraw 1/21.2 of that. IRS Publication 590 provides tables for these calculations.

The major pitfall for the recalculation method is that when one spouse dies, the minimum distribution must then be calculated based on the life expectancy of the remaining spouse only, boosting each year's distribution. When the second spouse dies, the estate must pay income tax on the remaining balance. Because of the tax advantages, many people want to preserve their retirement balances for as long as possible and this method works against that.

The second option, called "term-certain" because the term of the payout is set up front, is available only to those who elect it, in writing, before April 1 of the year after they turn 70½. Under term-certain, the couple aged 70 and 67 with a joint life expectancy of 22 years would merely subtract one year for each annual distribution. In the second year they would take 1/21, then 1/20, and so on. If one spouse dies, the distribution amount is still locked in. When the second dies, the estate continues to receive distributions over the term established up front, delaying tax on the money.

Goldberg claims that term-certain is always the best option. The minimum withdrawal is slightly larger initially, but there is no risk of having everything accelerated when one spouse dies. But other experts, like Tim Kochis, a financial planner in San Francisco, argue that recalculation fits the majority of taxpayers better chiefly because most people need the money in their retirement account as income during retirement.

To decide which method is best for you, think about your goals. Look at how much income you have for your retirement and where it will come from. Remember that you can always pull the money out faster than required. Minimum distributions simply define the *minimum* you are permitted to take. Penalties are stiff for those who take too little. You must forfeit 50 percent of the difference between the amount you withdraw and the minimum requirement, as well as pay tax on the withdrawal. Make this decision carefully and consult with an accountant if you need guidance or if you have a large balance.

LOOK AT SPOUSE'S RIGHTS

STEP

77

Spouses have special rights as beneficiaries of retirement accounts. After the death of the account holder, a spouse beneficiary at any age can either remain a beneficiary—leaving the account under the same name—or make the IRA his or her own.

If the spouse chooses to remain a beneficiary, he or she can ask for the money in the account to be paid out as a lifetime annuity. Or the surviving spouse can take the money out over the five years following the spouse's death. In either case, taxes would be due only when the money is received, and the 10 percent penalty assessed on people who take money out of these accounts before age 59½ would be avoided.

If, however, the spouse chooses to make the IRA his or her own, all IRA rules apply. For example, the account can be rolled over. Money can be added to it. But no money can be withdrawn until age 59½ without paying the 10 percent penalty.

That means that a spouse under age 59½ who wants to get the money out is better off remaining a beneficiary. A surviving spouse who plans to use the money for retirement would be better off claiming the IRA as his or her own. To do that, the spouse need only write to the bank or mutual fund company and claim the account.

For many people, the attraction of a retirement account is the ability to shelter income from taxes until retirement, when they will need the money to live on. But for retirees who do not need the money immediately, the accounts can continue to shelter the money until it must be withdrawn and taxes paid.

Once the account holder passes age 70½ and hits his required beginning date, some of the beneficiary designations cannot be changed. For instance, once the retirement account is in payout phase, the account holder cannot name a beneficiary that would stretch out that payout phase. So if a 70-year-old man has named his 67-year-old wife, he would not be permitted to change the beneficiary to his 10-year-old grandson *and* stretch the payment period once he had started taking minimum distributions. He is permitted to change the beneficiary but *not* to change the payment period.

Some experts believed that this same rule would apply to a spouse who inherited an IRA when she was past age 70½ and the IRA was already in payment status. According to this logic, the spouse would have no choice but to continue receiving distributions as scheduled under either the recalculation method or the term-certain method *(see **STEP 76**)*. However, in 1993, the Internal Revenue Service ruled that a spouse who is past age 70½ still has the option to claim the IRA as his or her own or to roll it over, the same two choices as a spouse at any other age. That gives the surviving spouse an opportunity to switch from the less favorable recalculation method to the term-certain method, stretching out the payout period and the tax deadline, if that is desired.

It also means the surviving spouse can choose a new beneficiary and stretch the payout period even further. Consider an IRA account holder who is 76 and has a 73-year-old wife as his beneficiary. They may have selected the term-certain method and have a remaining payout period of 15 years. If the husband died in 1997, the wife could claim the account as her own and name a new beneficiary. Her first required distribution date would be December 31, 1998. If she chooses a child or grandchild as beneficiary, she may be able to lengthen her own payout period and, if she chooses, to preserve more money for her heirs.

The rules that pertain to spouses are complex. If you inherit an IRA, get help from an expert if you're uncertain about what to do to preserve your options.

DON'T NAME A REVOCABLE
TRUST AS BENEFICIARY

STEP
78

When Dale R. Detlefs retired in 1992 as head of the Social Security division at William M. Mercer Inc., a consulting firm, he rolled his 401(k) money into an individual retirement account. Like many retirees, Detlefs would like to preserve as much money as possible for his children and grandchildren. Although he doesn't know how much he will need, he wants to keep his options open and to keep the tax deferral going on this money for as long as possible. "This constitutes a major part of my estate," he says. "If it's set up properly, you can keep the tax deferral going. If you do it wrong, the whole darn thing can become taxable."

When he went to a bank for advice, Detlefs was told to name a revocable living trust as the beneficiary of his IRA. By doing more research, he found that the revocable trust could have done exactly what he wanted to avoid: make all of the money taxable at his death. Among the biggest mistakes people make in retirement and estate planning is naming revocable trusts or their estates as beneficiaries of retirement money, experts say. "This is a disaster area," says Stuart Kessler, a partner at Goldstein Golub Kessler & Company, an accounting firm in New York. "Most people are absolutely unaware of how to set up beneficiary designations."

Many people, like Detlefs, want to leave retirement money in tax-deferred accounts for their children or grandchildren, provided they have enough money for themselves. But tax rules generally require that retirement money be used for retirement. Because the money in retirement accounts has never been taxed, the Internal Revenue Service takes the view that the sooner it comes out and is made taxable, the better.

A trust is an entity that owns and disposes of property through a trustee as directed by the grantor, or the person who sets up the trust. There are two broad types of trusts. One is revocable, meaning that the grantor is permitted to change or revoke the terms of the trust at any time during his lifetime. The other is irrevocable. When assets are transferred to an irrevocable trust, they cannot be reclaimed by the grantor.

The reasons for naming a revocable trust as beneficiary may sound convincing: Putting the account into such a trust allows the money to be managed by a trustee if the account holder becomes incapacitated. It also avoids probate. And the trustee can control the assets after the account holder dies. Likewise, the argument for naming the estate as beneficiary is that it allows the will to control the disposition of retirement assets. Otherwise, assets in retirement accounts pass outside the will.

The problem, though, is that withdrawals from retirement accounts are based on the life expectancy of the account holder and beneficiary. Neither an estate nor a revocable trust has a life expectancy. When the account holder calculates minimum distributions from the IRA, he must use his life expectancy alone, which speeds mandatory payouts. When another person is beneficiary, the account holder can calculate distributions based on their joint life expectancy. When the account holder dies, all the money is paid into the trust and becomes immediately subject to income tax.

Consider what happened to a client of Goldberg's whose husband had made a revocable trust beneficiary of his $300,000 IRA. The IRA was paid into the trust and taxed at 40 percent, leaving $180,000 for the spouse. Had he made the spouse beneficiary instead, she could have rolled the entire $300,000 into her own IRA and withdrawn it gradually over her lifetime.

DON'T USE A Q-TIP

STEP
79

Experts say that many families are being forced to pay thousands of dollars in estate taxes because they have been incorrectly advised to put their retirement money into a vehicle called a Q-Tip trust. If you think you might be one of them, read on.

Assets put into a Q-Tip, or a qualified terminable interest property trust, qualify for the unlimited marital deduction, which means no estate tax is due upon the death of the first spouse. The surviving spouse receives income from the trust, but the assets are safeguarded for the benefit of other heirs, usually children. Estate taxes are not due until the death of the second spouse.

The Q-Tip has become a very popular mechanism to provide income for a spouse but preserve the principal for the children from a prior marriage. The problem is that many people are being advised to include their retirement assets in these trusts. The distributions from many plans, like 401(k) plans and individual retirement accounts, fail to satisfy the requirements of a Q-Tip trust. If the trust requirements are not met, the Internal Revenue Service rules that estate taxes are owed on all the retirement plan money.

To qualify for the marital deduction on estate taxes, a Q-Tip must distribute all income to the surviving spouse at least once a year, the recipient must be a United States citizen, and the deceased must have designated a Q-Tip trust. Here's the problem: The payout options on 401(k) plans and IRAs are usually based on life expectancy. But if the retirement plan distributes less than its full annual income to the trust, all the money in the plan is disqualified for the marital deduction.

"A lot of people, just because they want to beat their second wife out of the money, are putting it into the Q-Tip trust," says Seymour Goldberg, an estate and tax attorney in Garden City, New York. "If they have $1 million in a retirement plan and it is disqualified for the marital deduction, the estate could end up with a whopping tax bill."

Suppose a $1 million retirement account is earning 7 percent, or $70,000 a year. If the Q-Tip is to qualify for the marital deduction, that $70,000 must go to the spouse as income. But the deceased spouse may have specified that the $1 million will be payable to the Q-Tip trust over 20 years, the joint life expectancy of the husband and wife. "What would happen is that the first year, $50,000 would go into the Q-Tip trust," Goldberg says. That does not meet the requirement for the Q-Tip and estate taxes would be owed on the entire $1 million.

Even if the distribution from the retirement plan happens to be more than the plan's annual income, that is not enough. To qualify for the marital deduction on estate taxes, the deceased must have specified that the IRA pay out all its income to the trust each year. "The test is not whether there is enough money from the IRA to meet the income requirement, but whether that option was actually selected," says Joshua Rubenstein, an estate partner with Rosenman & Colin, a New York law firm.

The trustee cannot change the retirement plan payout to make it conform to the trust's rules. Unless the IRA or 401(k) spells out this type of payout option and the participant elects it, estate taxes are due on all the retirement money in the trust. "It really has to say, 'In the event of death, all income from the account will be paid out each year to the Q-Tip trust,'" Goldberg says.

THINK ABOUT
ESTATE PLANNING

STEP

80

If you have more than enough money for your retirement and you want to leave some to your children—or even your grandchildren—you can get the most bang for your buck by leaving them money in a retirement account rather than taxable assets. That's thanks to the power of compounding on tax-deferred money. In fact, Seymour Goldberg argues that you can turn a $100,000 IRA into a $3 million windfall for a grandchild.

It takes some special planning to pass this money on, though. There is a special rule that governs retirement distributions if your beneficiary is not your spouse and that beneficiary is more than 10 years younger than you. In that case you must begin withdrawals from your retirement account when you turn 70½ based on what is called a minimum distribution incidental benefit (MDIB) table published by the Internal Revenue Service. This table calculates the withdrawals as if your beneficiary were only 10 years your junior.

For example, suppose 70-year-old Tom names his 35-year-old daughter, Jane, as beneficiary for his retirement account. The two have a joint life expectancy of 47.5 years. But the MDIB table calculates withdrawals as if Jane were 60, giving the two a joint life expectancy of 26.2 years. Then, when Tom dies, Jane can revert to her actual life expectancy to continue withdrawing the money. Likewise, if Tom names his 10-year-old granddaughter as beneficiary, their joint life expectancy is 71.8 years. Again, Tom must use the same 26.2 years when he begins withdrawing the money. But when Tom dies, his granddaughter can stretch the withdrawals out over her actual life expectancy. Even a small amount given to a young grandchild can grow to a substantial sum if it is left alone, without a bite for taxes. Of course, the grandchild must pay taxes when the money is withdrawn. Still, the gift will be much more significant than one made with after-tax dollars.

Some grandparents may want to split retirement money into several accounts, with the spouse as beneficiary of one and different beneficiaries—such as children and grandchildren—for the others. If you decide to pursue that course, you may calculate your minimum distribution and take the entire amount from just one account, leaving the others intact for beneficiaries.

Using retirement accounts to pass on money to grandkids is advantageous both because of the tax deferral and because money in a retirement account passes to the beneficiary outside a will, avoiding probate. However, the total amount that is passed to all of your grandchildren, whether in the form of a retirement account or not, cannot exceed $1 million. If it does, you must pay what is called a generation-skipping transfer tax on the excess.

Goldberg developed an irrevocable trust to receive money from a grandparent's IRA and pass it along to a custodial account for the grandchild. Here's how it works. Assume Tom leaves $100,000 in an IRA for his granddaughter, who has a life expectancy of 70 years at his death. The first year, $1,429 (1/70 of $100,000) goes into the trust from the IRA and then from the trust to a custodial account. Taxes are paid for the granddaughter based on the kiddie tax rules. The second year, the account balance is divided by 69, and so forth through the years.

Of course, the trustee could decide to speed up distributions at some point for college or a business opportunity for the child. But the advantage of the trust is that it allows the grandchild to defer tax—and continue accumulations—for as long as possible.

BEWARE OF PENSION MAX

STEP
81

One withdrawal option for your retirement money is an annuity, which pays
income for life. Many retirees like this
option because it eliminates their fear that
they will outlive their money. The arguments for and
against an annuity are a different matter. What we will
discuss here is a popular strategy called "pension max."

Let's assume that you have decided in favor of an
annuity. Now you must decide among several different payout options. If you choose a single life
annuity, you will receive income for your lifetime
only. When you die, the income stops. If you elect a
"joint and survivor" annuity, you would receive less initially but the benefit would continue for the lifetime
of your spouse. For example, the initial benefit might
be reduced to 75 percent or 50 percent and then your
spouse would continue to receive 100 percent of that
reduced benefit.

The pension max—or pension maximization—
strategy advocates electing the larger single-life
annuity and buying an insurance policy on the life of
the retiree, the proceeds of which would be turned
into an annuity to provide income for the spouse if
the retiree dies first.

Here is an illustration of how pension max might
work, provided by a financial planner. A teacher in
New York State retires at age 55. He can choose
$28,000 a year for the rest of his life or $21,000 a year
until both he and his spouse die.

If he elects the single benefit, he must protect his
spouse by buying a life insurance policy with a face
value of 10 times the annual benefit under the joint-
and-survivor option—or $210,000—to provide the
same protection for her. This planner recommends
a cash-value policy that would be paid up in seven to
10 years.

Such a policy—which has a level premium—might cost about $6,500 a year for 10 years, still leaving the retiree with $500 more than he would have had from the lower-paying survivor option. After 10 years, the retiree would have the extra $7,000 in benefits to spend each year.

It sounds good. But it doesn't necessarily work out that way, according to actuaries, who say pension max is generally a bad idea. One key reason is that the typical pension plan uses a more modest assumption about interest rates than does the typical insurance policy.

A pension plan calculates the survivor benefit by assuming that the money you forgo by not taking the single-annuity benefit will earn 5 to 8 percent until it must be paid out to your spouse, according to Ethan E. Kra, an actuary specializing in retirement issues. But the insurer may assume that the premium dollars you pay will grow at the rate of 9 or 10 percent a year so that the policy will be self-sustaining, requiring no further premium payments, in the prescribed period of seven to 10 years.

But the point at which the policy becomes self-sustaining is merely speculative. When interest rates go down, the value of the policy fails to meet the projections the company outlined. In that case, the policy-holder has three options: pay higher premiums, get less insurance, or drop the policy.

Nor does the pension max strategy take taxes into account. If you elect the single-benefit option, you must pay tax on the extra payments. Further, many companies subsidize the survivor's benefits, rather than just reducing them according to a formula.

Buying an insurance policy transfers the financial risk to you and your spouse. If you become ill, are moved to a nursing home, or don't keep up with the financial paperwork or premium payments, your spouse could be left with nothing.

COMPLETE A LIVING WILL

STEP

82

Longer life expectancies and medical "miracles" are creating new quality-of-life issues for retirees. In October 1998, a 1994 law in Oregon that permits physician-assisted suicide for chronically ill patients was upheld by the Supreme Court. Surely we will see more of these types of laws in the 21st century.

About 80 percent of Americans die in institutions, according to Choice in Dying, a nonprofit group based in New York. These sobering trends make it so important to have documents that appoint someone to make medical and financial decisions for you if you are unable to do so. It is as important as a traditional will.

A durable power of attorney appoints someone to make financial moves for you, such as signing your tax return or selling your car. To allow someone to make health care decisions, you need a medical directive, a living will, or medical power of attorney.

A federal law effective December 1, 1991, called the Patient Self-Determination Act, requires hospitals and other health care providers to give adults information when they are admitted about their rights to accept or refuse medical treatment and to prepare a document that will authorize someone else to make decisions for them.

Individuals have long had the right to refuse treatment, but until recently it was not clear whether they retained the right when they became incapacitated, according to Peter J. Strauss, a New York elder lawyer. "The question was, do you lose that right when you no longer have the ability to communicate because of incompetency or illness?"

In 1990, the Supreme Court upheld a ruling that found the state of Missouri was entitled to require "clear and convincing evidence" that Nancy Cruzan, who had been in a vegetative state since a 1983 automobile accident, would have wanted a feeding tube to be withdrawn under those circumstances.

"The Supreme Court said that you do not lose the right to refuse medical care when you become incapacitated," Strauss says. "However, the states have the right to lay down reasonable rules to determine what your wishes are."

Under the patient's rights law, those rules must be communicated to you. New York, like Missouri, requires "clear and convincing evidence" of the wishes of the patient. These wishes can be conveyed with a health care declaration or living will.

The living will drawn up by Strauss directs that life-prolonging medical treatments be discontinued if the patient is left "unable to communicate with others meaningfully" and "there is no reasonable prospect of recovery." It defines the medical treatments that should be discontinued, including "nutrition and respiration by artificial means." "In other words, if I am in a coma or vegetative state, I do not want any treatment," Strauss says.

Some people may want to specify that they would like any type of treatment that is available. "It's just as important to spell that out," Strauss says. "This is a choice issue. It is not a pull-the-plug issue."

Medical directives are not just for the elderly. Experts say everyone over the age of 18 should draw one up. "When my son turned 18, he thought the rites of passage were to get an earring and buy a lottery ticket," says Dee Lee, a financial planner in Harvard, Massachusetts. "I told him about registering with Selective Service and signing a health care proxy."

In many states, you can buy the necessary forms in a stationery store. You can also get them from a financial planner or from Choice in Dying.

TAKE ANOTHER LOOK
AT YOUR ESTATE PLAN

STEP 83 If you have anything special that you want to pass on to someone, you need a will outlining your wishes. If you have more than $600,000 in assets, you need an estate plan. It need not be complicated. But if you don't take the time to do it, much of the money you leave will go to pay estate taxes rather than to your heirs.

Many couples make the same mistake in estate planning: they hold all of their property jointly—or leave everything to each other in their wills. "Ninety percent of the wills I see are what are I call 'love me' wills," says Edward A. Slott, a certified public accountant in Rockville Centre, New York. "They say: 'I leave everything to you and you leave everything to me.'"

Any couple with a total estate of more than $600,000 may trigger unnecessary taxes by doing that. That's because they may not be able to take full advantage of the personal exemption from estate taxes as well as the unlimited marital deduction.

The exemption allows each person to pass on a specific amount of money tax-free to heirs other than a spouse during his or her lifetime or at the time of death. This "exclusion" from estate taxes is $600,000 in 1997. The Taxpayer Relief Act of 1997 raises the amount, gradually, beginning at $625,000 in 1998 and reaching $1 million in 2006. It also raised the exemption level for qualified family-owned businesses to $1.3 million beginning in 1998.

Estate taxes start at 37 percent of the amount that exceeds the allowed exclusion and go up to 55 percent. An unlimited amount may be passed on to a spouse who is an American citizen. (Noncitizens do not get this unlimited marital deduction.) When the second spouse dies, however, he or she has only the exclusion left to shield the remaining estate. So splitting the property between the spouses early on to take advantage of both their personal exemptions is the first step in a good estate plan. "Division of property is one of the keys to estate planning," Slott says. "Equalization of both spouses' estates will provide the lowest possible estate tax."

That way, couples with an estate of up to $1.2 million—or $2 million once the new law is fully phased in—can shield their property entirely from federal estate tax if they do a little planning. One way is to leave the amount of the exclusion to a child and the remainder to the spouse, thus taking advantage of the marital deduction as well as the spouse's own exemption.

Of course, a lot of couples with an estate that is just over $2 million do not want to give up so much at the first spouse's death. They might consider, instead, a trust that is referred to as a "credit shelter trust" or a "bypass trust." The trust makes use of the exempted amount and the remaining property passes to the spouse.

The surviving spouse can receive all the income from the trust. But the principal will go to the heirs at the death of the second spouse. Such a trust can be set up in your will so that the money goes into the trust at your death. A credit shelter trust could save the estate of a couple worth $1.2 million up to $235,000 in federal taxes, Slott says.

In order for this to work out, though, each spouse must hold separate property. "If you hold everything in joint name, there will be no money to fund the trust," says Joshua S. Rubenstein, an estates and trust partner at Rosenman & Colin in New York. "Joint property is never as good as property held in your own name."

PAY ATTENTION TO SPECIAL
RULES FOR NONCITIZENS

STEP 84

Many estate planning professionals fail to advise couples of the distinct rules for those who are not U.S. citizens. If both spouses are citizens, either can claim an unlimited marital deduction, which allows them to leave all their assets free of estate tax to each other. Citizens can also make unlimited gifts to spouses without incurring gift tax. But if one spouse is not a citizen, these exemptions are reduced.

"Planners often don't think to ask the question because the spouse speaks perfect English with no accent," says Alan Nadel, a partner at the Arthur Andersen & Company accounting firm in New York. That's the case with his wife, Yafa, who is an Israeli citizen. Estate planning is critical for her and others with substantial assets because the United States levies estate taxes on the assets of all citizens and domiciliaries, or people who make their home here. "We are the only country that does that," says John Dadakis, a partner at Rogers & Wells, a New York law firm.

Shortly after the unlimited marital deduction was added to estate tax laws in 1981, members of Congress began to worry that a spouse who was not a citizen would use the deduction to escape tax entirely and then take the money to another country. A spouse who is a citizen cannot skirt taxes that way. On the death of the second spouse, estate tax is owed on all assets above the unified credit, which is the amount Americans can give away or leave to heirs (besides spouses) free of federal gift and estate tax. The unified credit, or estate tax exclusion, is $600,000 for 1997 and will increase gradually to $1 million in 2006. Excess amounts are taxed from 37 percent to 55 percent.

Congress addressed what it considered the loop-hole for noncitizens in 1988, mandating that a U.S. citizen can leave only the amount of the unified cred-it free from tax to a noncitizen spouse. In addition, the citizen can make annual gifts as large as $100,000 to a noncitizen spouse without eating into the lifetime unified credit. If a resident, the surviving spouse then can make gifts or leave to heirs free from estate and gift tax the amount of the unified credit. If not a resi-dent, the spouse can leave only 10 percent of the uni-fied credit free from tax, or $60,000 for 1997.

The same law that took away the unlimited marital deduction provided a weak substitute called the qual-ified domestic trust. This type of trust bypasses estate taxes when a citizen dies and leaves an estate to a spouse who is not a citizen. But the terms of this trust are not as liberal as the qualified terminal property trust, or Q-Tip, used by citizens. With a Q-Tip, all trust income is paid to the surviving spouse. When the second spouse dies, the remainder is taxed in that person's estate.

Under the terms of a qualified domestic trust, sometimes called a Q-Dot, the first estate is left open. When the second spouse dies, the money left in the trust is taxed in the estate of the first to die. "Q-Dots are a very cumbersome device, but they are the only option for a surviving spouse who is not a U.S. citi-zen," says Joshua Rubenstein, a partner at Rosenman & Colin, a New York law firm.

Like other couples, a couple that includes a nonciti-zen should take care to split their assets equally. Dur-ing their lifetimes, they should make use of the $100,000 annual exclusion from gift taxes to make gifts that equalize their estates. If the estates are balanced, and each is under the amount of the unified credit, they can leave everything to the other free of tax.

TIE UP LOOSE ENDS

STEP
85

When her grandfather died, Shelley Freeman traveled from her home in New York to his home near Miami Beach to settle the estate. Although he had a valid will, specifying that assets were to be divided between his two children, it fell far short of answering all the questions that popped up. "The house was crammed with artwork—maybe 60 or 70 pieces—including two Chagalls," Freeman says. She wondered: What was the art worth? How should it be appraised? Should it be sold? "I finally looked up an appraiser in the Yellow Pages because I didn't know what else to do," she says.

As Freeman's experience points out, a will is essential, but it still may leave many matters for survivors to resolve. Additional written instructions can ease the burden on executors and others. Burial arrangements are a good example. "I had a big conflict when my grandparents died," Freeman says. "My father wanted them cremated. I wanted a rabbi to say Kaddish for them. I eventually won on that."

Freeman has a great deal of professional and personal experience in dealing with estates. She has been named executor of four estates for friends and family. And she served as director of personal financial planning for Shearson Lehman Brothers. Practicing what she preaches, she wrote her own will at age 35 and compiled a list of everything survivors might need to know, including insurance details, pension plan balances, and the names of her broker, accountant, and lawyer. Take a page out of Freeman's book and put together your own list of everything your executor needs to know.

For those who need a little push to collect a lifetime of records, the *Beneficiary Book* can help. It was written by Martin Kuritz, an estate planner for 30 years.

The handbook costs $30 plus $3 shipping and handling. A software program intended to be used with it sells for $25 (800-222-9125). Kuritz, who lives in Carlsbad, California, says he always found many missing pieces when he helped survivors deal with estates and came up with the idea of a book to encourage people to leave better information for their heirs.

Putting things in writing can help family members to accept your wishes, Kuritz says. For example, one client who was about to die wanted a $250 cremation. His wife was making plans for a lavish funeral. "When he put it in writing, she was not happy about it," Kuritz says. "But she knew that that was what he wanted."

A family needs only one *Beneficiary Book,* Kuritz says, but will have to spend several hours filling it out. Topics range from insurance and pension benefits to mundane matters like plumbers, repair and service people, computer passwords, dentists, and veterinarians. One section asks for a list of all money owed to debtors. Another asks for details about motor vehicles and valuables, including appraisals and receipts.

A couple of years ago, when Kuritz had finished writing the book, he and his wife were preparing to leave for vacation. To make sure their own affairs were in order, his wife filled out her portion of their personal book. Then she told him she wasn't going until he finished his part of the project. "She had completed her portion and she said I had to do my part of it before we left," Kuritz says. It took him about 12 hours.

These are the kind of tasks no one relishes. On the other hand, completing them can be valuable to you as well as invaluable to your heirs. You will get a sense—perhaps for the first time—of where your assets are, and you will have everything you need pulled together in one place. It will provide a good foundation for decision making.

LOOK AT DISCLAIMER WILLS

STEP 86 Most people never do the necessary planning to reduce the taxes on their estates for two reasons: They don't want to think about dying and they refuse to give away money just so their heirs will pay less tax. While dying is inevitable, parting with your money before death to reduce taxes is not. An alternative is a disclaimer will, which is typically used by a surviving spouse to disclaim part of an estate, put it in a trust, and shield it from taxes when it passes to the children of the couple. "Disclaimer wills are used for postmortem estate planning," says J. Stoddard Hayes Jr., a trust lawyer at Gollatz, Griffin & Ewing in West Chester, Pennsylvania. "They provide the ability to plan a person's estate after he is dead."

A disclaimer is simply a refusal to accept a gift of property. In 1976, when the federal estate and gift tax code was revised, a statute was added to explain when a disclaimer was valid. A disclaimer must be an unqualified refusal to accept a property transfer or gift, and must be made within nine months of the transfer, Hayes says. "Prior to 1976, disclaimers were a function of state law alone," he says. "Each state had a slightly different twist, and you never knew from one state to another whether you had a qualified disclaimer."

Most couples who write wills leave everything to the surviving spouse. But a couple with an estate of more than $600,000 in 1997 may trigger unnecessary taxes if they set up their wills that way because they will not take full advantage of the lifetime personal exemption of $600,000 and the unlimited marital transfer. Because couples often have estates of far less than $600,000 when they make their wills, they do not make provisions to maximize the use of that exemption. For couples with sizable assets, estate planners often recommend a bypass trust or credit shelter trust. When one spouse dies, $600,000 goes into the trust, making use of the lifetime exemption for each person. The surviving spouse receives the rest, making use of the unlimited marital deduction. The surviving spouse can receive all the income from the trust. But the principal goes to the heirs at his or her death.

A problem is that many couples worry that they will not have enough to live on if they commit $600,000 to such a trust. "Just because you have $1 million doesn't mean you want to put $600,000 of it into a credit shelter trust and lose access to it," says Joshua S. Rubenstein, a trust and estate partner at Rosenman & Colin in New York. "You may have $750,000 in the house and the rest in cash."

With a disclaimer will, spouses leave everything to each other, but specify what will happen to any property that is disclaimed. "What you say is: 'I give everything to Nancy. If Nancy should disclaim any part of this, it goes into a trust for her benefit and then ultimately to the kids,'" Rubenstein says. The surviving spouse has nine months from the date of death to decide whether to disclaim any of the property. Any amount may be disclaimed, but it will be free from estate taxes only up to $600,000 in 1997, an amount that increases gradually to $1 million in 2006.

The strategy does not work unless the will lays out specifically what will happen to the disclaimed property. In other words, the will must acknowledge the possibility of a disclaimer and address what will happen to property that is disclaimed. "You can use some wording that says if the spouse disclaims or predeceases me, then the property goes into a trust," Hayes says.

PART

7

403(b)s,
457 Plans,
ETC.

O VER THE PAST
15 years, 401(k) plans have become a household
word—even a cocktail party topic. These plans
have turned Americans who had never even heard
of a mutual fund into investors who hold
conversations about the merits of, say, Peter
Lynch's style as a growth investor at the Magellan
Fund versus the style of one of his various
successors like Jeff Vinik.

What to do, then, if you do not have a 401(k)
plan? There are millions of Americans who do
not have any kind of retirement plan at work.
Millions more work for themselves and have some
type of individual plan. But another huge group
of Americans qualify for salary reduction plans
at work that are similar to a 401(k) but with
slightly different provisions. Most of these plans
pre-date 401(k)s. They are called 403(b) plans,

457 plans, and sometimes "TDAs," for "tax-deferred annuities."

They bear enough resemblance to 401(k) plans to make many of the general rules of thumb worth knowing, particularly those in the investment area. Many 403(b) plans at hospitals, for example, offer the same broad range of investment options that you would expect to find in a good 401(k) plan. Yet these plans have some quirky differences that require some extra work on your part if you are to get the most out of them. In some cases, you may be able to squeeze an advantage out of a 403(b) that your friends can't manage with their 401(k) plans. Here are some of the things you should look into if you work at a nonprofit hospital, a school, a charitable foundation, a government agency, or some other employer that uses a salary reduction plan other than a 401(k).

BONE UP ON 403(B) PLANS

STEP

87

Nine million Americans who work for nonprofits and government agencies have a salary reduction plan at work that is similar to—but different from—a 401(k) plan.These school teachers, college professors, doctors, nurses, and government employees are permitted to contribute to a 403(b) plan, authorized by a different section of the Internal Revenue Code.

Section 403(b) was added to the Internal Revenue Code in 1958, a full 20 years before section 401(k), to permit employees at nonprofits and government agencies to set aside pretax money in an annuity contract offered by an insurance company. Thanks to its roots in the insurance industry, the 403(b) plan is often referred to as a TDA or "tax-deferred annuity."

In 1974, Congress added paragraph 7 to section 403(b). This newer provision permits employees to set up their retirement plans with mutual fund companies instead of insurance companies. "This section says that annuity contracts are not the only permissible investment vehicles for these plans," says Bob Walter, a consultant at Buck Consultants in Secaucus, New Jersey. Today participants in 403(b) plans can choose between annuities and mutual funds. But they cannot choose other options permitted in a 401(k) plan such as guaranteed investment contracts or individual stocks.

Participants in a 403(b) are permitted to contribute $9,500 a year to their plan, a number that is the same in 1997 as the 401(k) and that is indexed along with the 401(k) number. But unlike the 401(k), a 403(b) has a special catch-up provision that allows participants to contribute up to $12,500 a year for five years under certain specific circumstances. I spent a great deal of time trying to understand this catch-up provision so that I could explain it, but I could not find anyone who understood it well enough to explain it to me in plain English. Here is the best advice I can give you: If you have not contributed to a 403(b) when you were entitled to do so, or have contributed less than the maximum amount and now have extra money you would like to contribute, get the advice of an accountant on how to calculate it.

The pension simplification rules that were tacked on to the minimum wage bill passed in July 1996 provided that all nonprofits and government agencies will now be permitted to set up the more popular 401(k) plans if they choose. But that's not likely to happen. I called a half-dozen benefits consultants to find out if any of their clients planned to switch from 403(b) plans to 401(k)s. Not a single one planned to do so, chiefly because of the cost of setting up a new plan. Another snag is that there is no provision in the new law that allows 403(b) money to be rolled over to a 401(k). That means that an employer who chooses to set up a 401(k) would need to maintain both plans.

Those employers most likely to shift to a 401(k) are those that have both nonprofit employees and for-profit employees, such as a museum that runs a for-profit gift shop, according to Ethan Kra, chief actuary for retirement services at William M. Mercer Inc., benefits consultants in New York. Of course, those nonprofits that do not have plans may choose a 401(k) rather than a 403(b). And you can expect 403(b) plans to continue to grow more like the popular 401(k).

But if you have a 403(b) plan, chances are you will have it for a while. You may as well learn about it. Because they predate the Employee Retirement Income Security Act (ERISA, the pension law that established rules and regulations to govern private pension plans, including such things as vesting requirements and plan design), the rules for 403(b) plans are often looser than those for 401(k) plans. That means that you must really dig in and take responsibility for your plan if you are to get the most out of it.

FIND OUT WHAT TYPE
OF PLAN YOU HAVE

STEP 88 ERISA, or the Employee Retirement Income Security Act of 1974, requires that employers be prudent and vigilant in selecting, maintaining, and reviewing retirement plan investments. All 401(k) plans are governed by ERISA. But employers who sponsor 403(b) plans have a choice about whether to comply with ERISA or not. About half do so. Employees who participate in non-ERISA plans must do more work to make certain they choose a good plan and make good investment choices.

An employer that sponsors an ERISA plan chooses a vendor for a 403(b) plan in much the same way as 401(k) sponsors do. William M. Mercer's Ethan Kra refers to the 403(b) ERISA plan as a plan with a capital P because the employer takes charge of the plan. Even government employers, who are exempt from ERISA, can put together this type of plan. The employer provides educational materials like those offered in a 401(k) plan as well as a summary plan description. The employer may provide a matching contribution, too. And the employer must file a form 5500, which is an annual form that must be sent to the Internal Revenue Service for every qualified plan.

Many other employers leave it totally up to employees to decide whether or how they will invest their 403(b) money. These employers simply agree to withhold the money from your salary and to send it to the investment company of your choice. They have no responsibility for the choice you make. "They take a purely passive role and just tell employees to bring them the salary reduction agreement and they will send the money wherever the employee wants it to go," says Bob Walter of Buck Consultants. Kra calls this a plan with a small p because it has few boundaries.

For example, Kra's wife works in a private school where she was told she could invest retirement money wherever she liked provided she collected and filled out the forms and turned them in. "The employer has no responsibility other than forwarding the payroll deduction and filling out the W-2 properly," Kra says.

From the employer's point of view, the second type of plan can be very appealing because there are no responsibilities, fiduciary or otherwise. But from your perspective as the employee, this type of plan is appealing only if you know a fair amount about both investing and retirement vehicles. The plans in this category fit the old saw about insurance policies: These 403(b) plans are sold, not bought. The same insurance agents who push life insurance policies call teachers and others who qualify for 403(b) plans and try to sell them on an annuity product, usually without laying out the pros and cons.

I've talked with dozens of people who bought these plans—many of them teachers—without knowing exactly what they'd purchased. Most simply referred to their plan as a "TDA" for tax-deferred annuity. That is a recipe for disaster. If your employer is not involved in monitoring your plan, you must monitor it yourself.

Because many of the 403(b) products have surrender charges, it is critical to decide which type of product you want before you buy it. Be careful, too, that you check the various provisions of the agreement you enter into. Many of the annuity products lock you in for life. Once you buy the annuity, you must use it to accumulate your retirement money and then, once retired, you must accept the terms of that company's annuity payout.

Check these provisions before you start contributing to a 403(b). If you already have a plan and you discover that its terms are unattractive, be sure to look at the surrender fee before you decide to get out of the plan.

COMPARE 403(B) AND 403(B) 7

STEP
89

Today it is widely accepted among financial professionals that putting an annuity inside a retirement account is a bad idea. That's because an annuity provides one layer of tax deferral—at a cost—and a retirement account provides another. Yet the basic 403(b) plan provides for exactly that.

Worse yet, although a deferred annuity and an immediate annuity need not be inextricably intertwined, that is often the case for 403(b) products sold by insurance companies. For instance, the contract that a 25-year-old teacher buys may be binding for life. Not surprisingly, many of the contracts with those kinds of handcuffs do not provide particularly generous payout benefits.

An annuity is a tax-deferred investment that can be offered only by an insurance company. It typically has two phases. During the accumulation phase, the account holder can contribute money that grows without a bite for taxes. The 403(b) plan adds a second advantage during the accumulation phase: The contributions can be made pretax.

The second phase of an annuity is the payout phase. The insurance company promises that it will pay you money for the rest of your life—or that you will never run out of income. Legally, only an insurance company can make this promise because there is an element of insurance involved in figuring your life expectancy and guaranteeing that you will have income for life.

It is possible to buy these two elements separately. For instance, you could buy an annuity to save money for retirement and then take the money in a lump sum once you reach retirement age. Or you could save money in some other type of account, like an individual retirement account, and then buy an annuity that pays income for life once you retire. But many of the 403(b) annuity contracts do not permit that flexibility. They lock you into the plan for life. When you see a contract that requires you to stick with the same insurer while you accumulate the money and when you get the payment, you should assume it will not be to your advantage.

In 1974, Congress added paragraph 7 to section 403(b). This later provision permits employees to set up their retirement plans with mutual fund companies instead of insurance companies. Employees who must choose between these two types of vendors should think about whether they want a pure investment or guaranteed retirement income. Both products might include mutual funds as an investment option. But the insurance company product will wrap an annuity around the mutual funds at an additional cost. "There will be one charge for the mutual fund and one for the annuity wrapper," says Ethan Kra. "The two sets of fees make some annuities very expensive."

Mutual funds come in two varieties—those with commissions and those without commissions. But all annuities have some kind of load. "The load may be buried inside the annuity interest rate," Kra says. "But it's there." In other words, the load may be paid to the broker up front and then the insurance company recovers it by shaving something off the interest that is credited to account holders. "If you want to get out of the annuity, it may have a back-end charge," Kra says.

Because many of the 403(b) products have surrender charges, it is critical to decide which type of product you want before you buy it. Be careful, too, that you check the various provisions of the agreement you enter into. In some cases, 403(b) rules are "looser" than 401(k) rules in ways that work to the participants' advantage. But some vendors do not provide these advantageous options.

LOOK CAREFULLY AT THE
WITHDRAWAL RULES

STEP 90

Taxpayers make plenty of mistakes when taking withdrawals from retirement accounts, even when the rules are fairly well publicized. Imagine what can happen, then, with 403(b) plans, where the rules are practically a federal secret. When these plans were first set up, there were no rules whatsoever on withdrawing the money. Perhaps the government wasn't so concerned, reasoning that, if you put the money away for retirement, you'd take it out once you retired. Some of the rules that have evolved are more liberal than those for 401(k) plans. Unfortunately, they are difficult to find. That means those who find out about them can take advantage of them and the rest of us can't!

During your working years, you will probably be most interested in whether—and how—you can get money out of your plan. As with other retirement plans, the 403(b) rules now impose a 10 percent penalty on money that is withdrawn before age 59½. However, most 403(b) sponsors observe the same hardship rules that were written for 401(k) plans. That means, for example, that you could get your money out without a penalty if you suffered a disability or if you needed it to pay college bills for your child *(see **STEP 23** for hardship withdrawals.)*

The more interesting rules, though, are those that apply to mandatory withdrawals during retirement. Many people with other assets want to leave money in their retirement plans for as long as possible to continue tax deferral. In 1973, the IRS said that more than 50 percent of the money should be taken out of a 403(b) plan during a participant's lifetime. Actuarial tables were drawn up that provided a framework for withdrawals, but there was no mandatory starting point.

In the late 1970s, IRS actuaries informally agreed that age 75 "might be a good starting point," according to an IRS spokesperson. That age was then mentioned in private letter rulings, which are an IRS response to a question put by a taxpayer. A private letter ruling is intended only for the taxpayer who requests the ruling. The age 75 starting date was never included in regulations or other guidelines.

Then along came the Tax Reform Act of 1986. Among other things, the act required that 403(b) plans be governed by the minimum distribution rules in effect for other pension plans, like 401(k)s and IRAs. But the 1986 law made a distinction for the "old money" in 403(b) plans, saying these dollars could be withdrawn on the basis of the "old rules," which were not further defined. Most pension experts—and many vendors—concluded that the 1986 law meant for age 70½ to be the mandatory start-up point for both old and new money.

But the IRS acknowledged—at least to me—that it meant for age 75 to be the beginning date for old money. Only those plan participants who knew about this obscure rule—and who had a plan that permitted it—would be allowed to take advantage of it, though.

A better-known law that became effective in November 1989 and was made retroactive to 1986 provided that employees who continue to work in government or church jobs need not withdraw the "new money" until age 70½ or retirement, whichever is later. The 1996 pension simplification law broadened this to all qualified plan participants. That's another example, though, of the different kinds of rules that apply to 403(b)s. It's worth your time to research the specifics.

There's something to be said, too, for using a vendor familiar with the market. For example, when I was researching the age 75 rule, the only person I found who knew about it was a pension attorney at TIAA-CREF, which specializes in 403(b) plans.

BEWARE OF THE
403(B)–KEOGH PITFALL

STEP

91

Doctors, professors, and others who contribute to a 403(b) retirement plan at a nonprofit hospital, school, or other organization and then contribute to a separate retirement plan of their own, like a Keogh plan for the self-employed, may bump up against some unexpected obstacles.

That's because the contribution limits on the two plans can overlap. For a professional who has a 403(b) plan, the retirement vehicle used by nonprofit groups, the rules are quite strict. A big contribution to another plan can preclude any participation in the 403(b) plan. The 403(b) is the only retirement plan that is offset by contributions to all other retirement plans.

The annual limit on a 403(b) plan contribution is generally $9,500, although other factors may raise or lower it for an individual. The annual limit for many types of retirement plans, like Keogh accounts, is $30,000. That $30,000 limit supersedes the 403(b) limit. So a professor or university administrator who has self-employment income from consulting and contributes $30,000 to a Keogh plan cannot contribute at all to a 403(b) plan. To contribute $9,500 to the 403(b) he would have to keep his Keogh contribution to $20,500. "The rules apply to those who control more than 50 percent of their own company," says Dick Wickersham, technical adviser for employee plans at the Internal Revenue Service.

The situation is quite different for an executive at a corporation. He can contribute fully to a 401(k) plan or any other pension plan offered by his employer. And if he reports self employment income for consulting or serving on a board of directors, for example, he can contribute a portion of that money to a

Keogh self-retirement plan as well. "These are long-standing regulations," says Evelyn Petchek, director of employee plans at the IRS. "They are part of the statutes governing employee plans."

Yet most of the people affected are unaware of the rules, financial advisers say. When Seymour Goldberg, a lawyer at Goldberg & Ingber in Garden City, New York, and an expert on retirement plans, speaks to groups of doctors or professors, he typically asks how many put money into 403(b) plans. Not surprisingly, all of them do. Then he asks how many have Keogh plans. Perhaps a quarter of them do, Goldberg says.

Professionals who contributed the maximum for many years could have $600,000 to $700,000 in a 403(b) plan, Goldberg says. If these same people made the maximum Keogh contributions, all of their 403(b) money could be deemed immediately taxable by the IRS. "It depends on just how tough the IRS wants to be," Goldberg says.

In the mid '90s, the IRS began to audit 403(b) plans because the agency found what Petchek calls "a disturbing level of noncompliance" in these plans. At about the same time, the IRS began looking at returns of individuals who took a Keogh deduction on their 1040 to "see whether they complied with all the regulations," Petchek says. Although the IRS was not specifically searching for taxpayers who contributed to both types of plans, "obviously, if we are doing an exam of 403(b) plans and related Keogh issues come to our attention, we will not turn our back on it," Petchek says.

The bottom line is that a doctor who works at a nonprofit hospital with a 403(b) plan and who contributes $30,000 to a Keogh plan from private practice cannot contribute to the 403(b). If the doctor worked at a for-profit hospital, he could put money in the company 401(k) plan up to its limit while continuing his $30,000 Keogh contribution.

WATCH OUT FOR 457 PLANS

STEP

92

The tax code has its twists and turns. And it seems to abandon some taxpayers on the sharp curves. Those who work for a government agency or a nonprofit organization whose only retirement plan option is what is called a Section 457 plan cannot be blamed for counting themselves in that group.

Section 457 plans are one type of nonqualified retirement plan, which means they are unfunded and unregulated, like the supplemental plans set up for top corporate executives. But there are two important differences: In most cases 457 plans are pensions for the rank and file, rather than for high-paid executives. And, in most cases, the money that goes into the plans represents salary deferrals by the employee rather than a contribution by employers.

In that sense, they are the worst of both worlds. Employees are setting aside their own money for retirement. Yet they do not have the security of knowing that it will be there when they retire. The money in these plans can be taken by creditors of the employer—or even by the employer itself.

The 457 refers to the section of the tax code that lays out the rules for these plans. Prior to 1978, when section 457 was written, public employees could defer a virtually unlimited amount of their salary and let it grow in a tax-deferred plan. Policy makers saw that as a problem. In private companies, which pay tax on their earnings, there is a reason to limit tax deferrals to employees. If the employee defers income—and does not pay tax on it—the company cannot take a tax deduction either.

But because government entities and nonprofit organizations don't pay tax, there isn't the same kind of tug and pull. The result: "The government thought it was losing a lot of revenue here," says Allen Steinberg, a consultant at Hewitt Associates, a benefits firm in Lincolnshire, Illinois. So section 457 was written to place limits on these tax-deferred plans.

Consultants say that most participants do not understand the risks of 457 plans, which are offered by 95 percent of government organizations, according to a survey by Foster Higgins, benefits consultants. Those who do understand may decide to stay in the plan anyway, especially if it is the only one available through their employer. But others may decide to cut back the level of their contributions or not participate at all if they are concerned about their employer's financial health. They may put their money instead into a deductible IRA, an annuity, or even a savings account.

Consider what happened to employees of Orange County, California, in 1994 when that county filed for bankruptcy protection. They were told that they might get just 90 percent of the money that they had invested in their 457 plan.

Some nonprofits—like charitable and religious groups—are eligible for the better-known (and better-protected) 403(b) plans. But many are not. "There are chambers of commerce, sports associations, state and county governments, and a lot of other groups that can have a 457 but cannot have a 403(b) plan," says Michael Footer, a principal in the Richmond office of William M. Mercer Inc., benefits consultants.

Often, participants do not understand the limitations of these plans until it is too late. For instance, rollovers to IRAs are not permitted from these plans. That means a civil servant who retires in her fifties must pay tax immediately. She might have the option of leaving the money in the plan until age 65. But given that it is not set aside in an account with her name on it, that is not appealing. Loans are not available from the plans, either. Nor do they offer the range of investment options of a typical 401(k) plan.

PART

8

Sample
PORTFOLIOS

HEREVER you are in your career, you should make your 401(k) plan the core of your investment portfolio. But let's back up a moment. Do you have an investment portfolio? Can you describe what's in it? To many people, the word "portfolio" itself is intimidating. All it really means, though, is a collection of assets—securities and other investments such as stocks, bonds, gold, art, and real estate. The assets you buy and the way you combine them in a group will determine the investment return you achieve and that will largely determine whether you are able to accomplish your financial goals. You need to build a portfolio in a coherent way, with your 401(k) as the centerfold.

You undoubtedly own some investments. You may own a home. Perhaps you own some mutual funds. Maybe you've invested money in one of your passions, like fine art or tribal rugs. These various assets and investments represent part of your balance sheet. But a true investment "portfolio" should be more than just a list of investments. Some thought should be given to how these investments fit together and work together as a team.

Unfortunately, most people don't spend much time on that part of it. They buy mutual funds, stocks, and other investments haphazardly, based on tips from friends or recommendations from brokers. If they get a year-end bonus, they buy a fund—or perhaps they take a vacation! If it's April 15 and IRA time, they buy another fund. Then they read that a hot fund is about to close to new investors, and they jump in with their money before the deadline. What they end up with is a grab-bag. How it will perform is anybody's guess. My guess is the results will be disappointing.

Successful investing requires a plan. It requires discipline. You must be methodical if you are to develop an investment portfolio. Instead of buying this fund or that, investors should start with a list of asset classes. That sounds jargony. But all it really means is different types of investments, like large company stocks, small company stocks, foreign stocks, bonds, real estate, gold.

The point of having a portfolio is to diversify. Remember, the investment markets are cyclical. Some asset categories will do better in a given year, some will do worse. The next year they may change places. Professional investors endlessly attempt to qualify and quantify these movements in the market. But the fact of the matter is this: The mystery and unpredictability of the markets are what provide their rewards. If the market were predictable, it would provide minimal, money-market–type returns. So when you set up your portfolio, you must stretch it across different asset classes and then be prepared to sit tight. When one class outperforms, you will have that in your portfolio. You'll have the one that underperforms as well. But they will balance each other out. You must wring the emotion from your investing and resist the urge to try to move your assets to the current top performer.

That's exactly what professional investors do. Take Harold Evensky, for example. Evensky, a financial planner and investment manager in Coral Gables, Florida, who also happens to be chairman of the board of governors for certified financial planners as well as an engineer educated at Cornell University, looks at a portfolio purely in terms of the potential return and the level of risk, which he measures by estimating a worst-case scenario for that particular group of assets. The latest trends, news about hot stocks, sizzling sectors of the economy, or predictions that the market will plunge never turn Evensky's head.

We asked Evensky to set up model 401(k) portfolios for investors with varying risk tolerances from very low to very high. He used these 10 asset classes:

1 **Money market fund or short-term bonds with maturities of one to three years;**

2 **Short- to medium-term bonds with maturities of three to five years;**

3 **Medium-term bonds with maturities of five to 10 years;**

4 **A large-company stock index fund like the Vanguard 500 Index;**

5 **A large-company fund that uses a value approach to investing;**

6 **A large-company fund that uses a growth approach;**

7 **A small-company value fund;**

8 **A small-company growth fund;**

9 **An international fund that invests in developed countries;**

10 **An international fund that invests in emerging markets.**

If you have a 401(k) plan, like the employees at Chrysler Corp. do, that allows you to pick from virtually any available mutual fund, you will have no trouble finding these funds for your portfolio. If you have more limited choices, you might find you need to collapse some of these categories. For example, you might use these five:

1 **A short-term bond or fixed income fund;**

2 **A medium-term bond fund;**

3 **A large-company fund;**

4 **A small-company fund;**

5 **An international fund.**

Some 401(k) participants might find that they do not have even that many options. Suppose that you, like Brian Ternoey, a consultant at Foster Higgins, find that you have only two options in your plan: a fixed income option and an equity or stock option. You can still use Evensky's allocations. But you must combine all his fixed income or bond allocations into just one asset class and then combine all his equity options for your second fund. If your plan has limited options like that, you should aim to create an investment portfolio outside your 401(k) plan adding an international fund and a small-company stock fund.

Evensky set up 14 portfolios (I've given them names here) based on these asset classes, ranging from conservative to aggressive. For each portfolio, he provides an estimated real rate of return, which is the return after inflation. He also provides a measure of estimated risk. He does this by indicating the risk in the short term as Low (L), medium (M), or High (H) and then risk in the long term with the same measures.

STOCKS-BE-DAMNED (PORTFOLIOS 1-3)

PORTFOLIO 1: Seventy-two percent of this portfolio is in fixed income. It has low risk in both the short term and long term. Here's what it looks like:

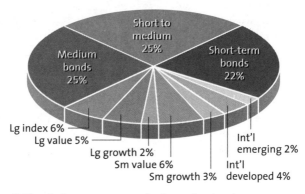

Estimated average annual return: 3 percent
Worst-case scenario: -4 percent in one year

Finally, he gives what he considers a worst-case scenario loss figure for each portfolio. This number, which is a percentage, is meant to indicate what Evensky thinks that portfolio might possibly be down in a 12-month period. He figures that in nine out of 10 years, this is the worst you could expect from this collection of assets. That doesn't mean it's the most the portfolio could ever lose in a day or a week. It's the worst loss over a 12-month period. So suppose the stock market crashes on January 2, 1998. Fast forward to January 2, 1999. With portfolio No. 1, his most conservative portfolio, Evensky estimates that the worst case is that your entire portfolio might be down 4 percent. In contrast, with portfolio 14, you might be down 35 percent a year after the crash.

With this in mind, let's take a look at his portfolios.

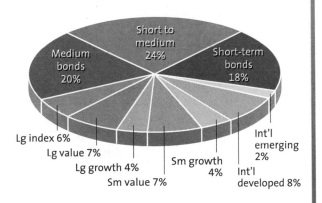

PORTFOLIO 2: We're taking one tiny step up here in terms of risk. This portfolio also has low risk in both the short term and long term.

Short to medium 24%

Medium bonds 20%

Short-term bonds 18%

Lg index 6%
Lg value 7%
Lg growth 4%
Sm value 7%
Sm growth 4%
Int'l developed 8%
Int'l emerging 2%

Estimated average annual return: 3.5 percent
Worst-case scenario: -7 percent

STOCKS-BE-DAMNED (CONT'D)

PORTFOLIO 3 carries medium risk in the short term and low risk in the long term.

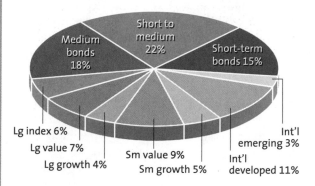

Short to medium 22%
Medium bonds 18%
Short-term bonds 15%
Lg index 6%
Lg value 7%
Lg growth 4%
Sm value 9%
Sm growth 5%
Int'l developed 11%
Int'l emerging 3%

Estimated average annual return: 4 percent
Worst-case scenario: -9 percent

SPLIT PERSONALITY (PORTFOLIOS 4 & 5)

PORTFOLIO 4 also has medium risk in the short term and low risk over the long term.

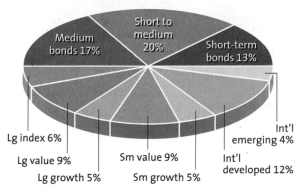

Short to medium 20%
Medium bonds 17%
Short-term bonds 13%
Lg index 6%
Lg value 9%
Lg growth 5%
Sm value 9%
Sm growth 5%
Int'l developed 12%
Int'l emerging 4%

Estimated average annual return: 4.3 percent
Worst-case scenario: -10 percent

PORTFOLIO 5 is medium risk in short term and low risk over the long term.

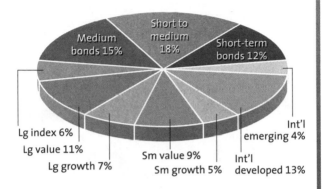

Estimated average annual return: 4.5 percent
Worst-case scenario: -11 percent

TWO TOES IN THE WATER (PORTFOLIOS 6 & 7)

PORTFOLIO 6 is medium risk in both short and long term.

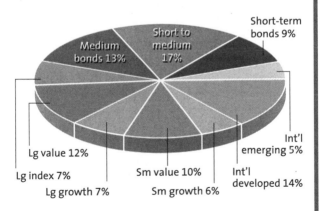

Estimated average annual return: 4.8 percent
Worst-case scenario: -13 percent

TWO TOES IN THE WATER (CONT'D)

PORTFOLIO 7 is high risk in the short term and medium risk in the long term.

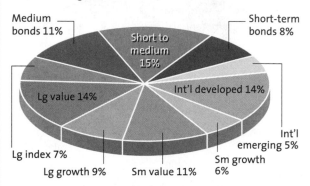

Estimated average annual return: 5 percent
Worst-case scenario: -14 percent

JUMPED IN WITH BOTH FEET (PORTFOLIO 8)

PORTFOLIO 8 is high risk in the short term and medium risk in the long term.

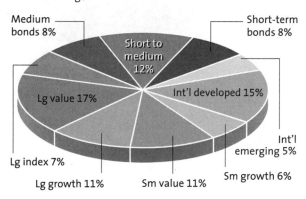

Estimated average annual return: 5.3
Worst-case scenario: -16

"EXTREME INVESTING" (PORTFOLIOS 9-14)

Portfolios 9 through 14 are all high risk in both short and long term. In fact, on his fancy computer-generated model portfolios, Evensky prints out these six portfolios in red lest anyone miss the potential risks.

PORTFOLIO 9

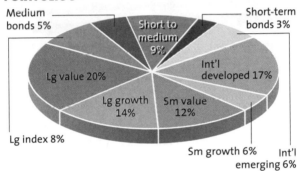

Medium bonds 5%
Short to medium 9%
Short-term bonds 3%
Lg value 20%
Int'l developed 17%
Lg growth 14%
Sm value 12%
Lg index 8%
Sm growth 6%
Int'l emerging 6%

Estimated average annual return: 5.5
Worst-case scenario: -20

PORTFOLIO 10

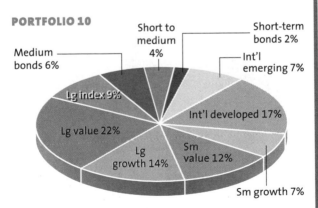

Short to medium 4%
Short-term bonds 2%
Medium bonds 6%
Int'l emerging 7%
Lg index 9%
Int'l developed 17%
Lg value 22%
Lg growth 14%
Sm value 12%
Sm growth 7%

Estimated average annual return: 5.8 percent
Worst-case scenario: -22 percent

"EXTREME INVESTING" (CONT'D)

PORTFOLIO 11

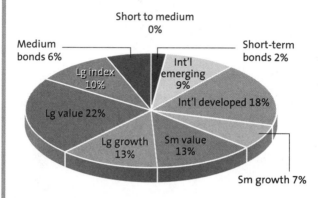

Short to medium 0%
Medium bonds 6%
Short-term bonds 2%
Lg index 10%
Int'l emerging 9%
Int'l developed 18%
Lg value 22%
Lg growth 13%
Sm value 13%
Sm growth 7%

Estimated average annual return: 6 percent
Worst-case scenario: -24 percent

PORTFOLIO 12

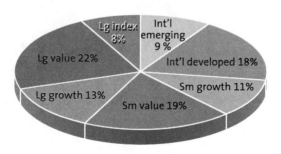

Medium bonds 0%
Short to medium 0%
Short-term bonds 0%
Lg index 8%
Int'l emerging 9 %
Lg value 22%
Int'l developed 18%
Sm growth 11%
Lg growth 13%
Sm value 19%

Estimated average annual return: 6.5 percent
Worst-case scenario: -27 percent

PORTFOLIO 13

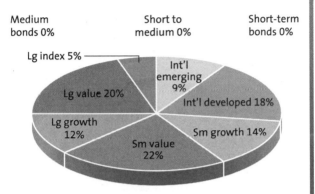

Medium
bonds 0%

Short to
medium 0%

Short-term
bonds 0%

Lg index 5%
Int'l emerging 9%
Lg value 20%
Int'l developed 18%
Lg growth 12%
Sm growth 14%
Sm value 22%

Estimated average annual return: 7 percent
Worst-case scenario: -31 percent

PORTFOLIO 14

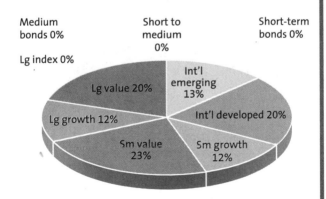

Medium
bonds 0%

Short to
medium
0%

Short-term
bonds 0%

Lg index 0%
Int'l emerging 13%
Lg value 20%
Int'l developed 20%
Lg growth 12%
Sm value 23%
Sm growth 12%

Estimated average annual return: 7.5
Worst-case scenario: -35

RESOURCES

HERE IS CERTAINLY no end of resources to help you plan your retirement and to invest the money you need to get there. Here are some books, magazines, newsletters, and Web sites that I think you might find helpful or interesting.

ABOUT 401 (K) PLANS

Building Your Nest Egg With Your 401(k), by Lynn Brenner (Investors Press Inc., 1995) is a colorful, appealing, accessible book that answers all the questions you might have on how the 401(k) plan works.

The 401(k) Association in Cross Fork, Pennsylvania, is a membership group of employee participants that aims to promote and protect 401(k) plans. Membership dues are $35 the first year and $25 in subsequent years.

R. Theodore Benna, who heads the group, is the man who developed the first 401(k) plan.

The group is also a good source of help in setting up low-cost 401(k) plans for small companies. Benna sets up 401(k)s at a cost of $1,000 plus an annual fee of just $700 for 10 employees and $10 per person for each additional employee. Benna provides all the compliance testing, communications, and reports—the stuff that everybody hates to deal with because it's tough and there's no money to be made in it. The business can set up its 401(k) wherever it chooses—Vanguard Group, Charles Schwab & Co., Fidelity Investments, and so forth (814-435-1300; 1117 Pine Hill Road, Cross Fork, PA 17729).

The 401 (k) Plan Management Handbook: A Guide for Sponsors and Their Advisors, by Jeffrey

M. Miller and Maureen M. Phillips (Irwin Professional Publishing, 1996) is a book is written for the sponsor rather than the participant. But it's written in English. If you have questions about what the other
players are doing in the 401(k) marketplace—that is
the government and the employers who sponsor
plans—this is a good place to get answers.

BASIC PERSONAL FINANCE

IF YOU HAVE DEBT/CREDIT PROBLEMS, you need
The Ultimate Credit Handbook, by Gerri Detweiler,
(Plume/Penguin, 1997; $12.95). Detweiler, the for-
mer executive director of BankCard Holders of America, a consumer group, provides a blueprint for getting out of debt and staying debt-free.

Her friend, Marc Eisenson, wrote *The Banker's Secret*
(Villard Books, 1991; $14.95), making the argument
for paying off your mortgage. It's a good one. Eisenson paid off his own mortgage at the age of 27 and
then semiretired from his construction business and
began writing, creating the life he wanted for himself
in the Hudson Valley, where he gardens and generally enjoys himself. Eisenson and his partner, Nancy
Castleman, also publish the *Banker's Secret Newsletter,*
Box 78, Elizaville, NY 12523, and answer questions on
the Banker's Secret Hotline: 914-758-1400.

Estate planning is a tough area. It's daunting and
boring at the same time. But doing a good job here
can make a huge difference for your heirs. One of
the best ways to get organized is with *The Beneficiary
Book,* written by Martin Kuritz, an estate planner who
says he always found missing pieces whenever he
helped survivors deal with estates. He wrote the book
to encourage people to leave better information for
their heirs.

The handbook costs $30, plus $3 shipping and
handling. A software program intended to be used
with it sells for $25 (800-222-9125).

INVESTING

MORNINGSTAR, THE CHICAGO rating service, is the best source of information on mutual funds for consumers (800-876-5005). The company's flagship product, which is called *Morningstar Mutual Funds,* is a loose-leaf binder that includes one page on each of the 1,500 funds covered. This service now costs $395 a year, which is a steep price for individual investors. It also provides more information than most need. In 1995, Morningstar introduced a shorter version that includes 700 no-load and low-load funds. This product, at $145 a year, is a much better choice for investors who plan to pick their own funds.

Both publications carry the same analysis. You will be able to see how big the fund is in terms of assets under management, and the net asset value. Each fund is compared with a market index, such as the Standard & Poor's 500 Stock Index for large-company stocks or the Russell 2000 for small-company stocks. The analysis includes year-by-year performance numbers, going back 10 years, which allows you to see how volatile the fund is. For example, if a fund is up 50 percent one year and down 30 percent the next, you may decide that's too much movement for you.

The performance graph marks changes in portfolio managers with an arrow. The fund's long-term record is meaningless if it has a brand-new portfolio manager. I look at the style box, a nine-square grid that shows whether the fund buys small, medium, or large companies and whether it is growth or value-oriented. I look at the style history, too, to see if the manager has been consistent or if he skips from one style to another. The 200-word analyses are terrific and accessible even to beginners.

I look, too, at the star rankings, which award a fund zero to five stars. The star system is based largely on the fund's recent past performance, so looking only at five-star funds is not a good way to pick a winner. There are good reasons to consider funds with lower rankings. For example, a good manager's style may have been out of favor and be due for a comeback.

Just because a fund is not yet rated by Morningstar doesn't mean you shouldn't buy it. Morningstar waits until a fund is at least three years old. An analysis may be included on a new fund, but it will indicate that it is "not rated." Morningstar sends updates to the volume every two weeks, with commentaries by editors and surveys or studies the company has done. These commentaries provide some of the best thinking available on what is happening in the mutual fund world. *Morningstar Mutual Funds* can be found in most libraries.

Really serious investors swear by Morningstar OnDisc, a CD-ROM that includes all the mutual funds available and allows investors to sort funds, set up portfolios, compare one fund to another, and so forth. The CD-ROM costs $295. If you want monthly updates, it costs $495. A demonstration disk is available for $5.

Look in the library, too, for the *Value Line Mutual Fund Survey*. *Value Line* is the traditional source of research on individual stocks, and the mutual fund service was introduced to compete with Morningstar's service.

The American Association of Individual Investors (AAII), based in Chicago, provides excellent information for investors in its monthly journal, as well as free investment seminars for members. Some of the best investment minds in the country agree to speak at these seminars because they believe in helping to educate investors. To join, send $49 to AAII, 625 North Michigan Avenue, Chicago, IL 60611.

Do you need an investment newsletter? If you're just picking mutual funds for your 401(k) plan, perhaps not. If you've been bitten by the investing bug and want to learn more, subscribe to the monthly *Morningstar Investor,* available for $79 a year. Look here for information on funds that plan to close or reopen, portfolio manager changes, and discussions of different investing styles. The centerpiece of this newsletter is the Morningstar 500, a list of 500 funds the rating agency believes have special merit.

The No-Load Fund Investor, written by Sheldon Jacobs, a longtime observer of the mutual fund industry, is also well worth the $99 subscription price for investors who want no-load funds. Jacobs includes news of new funds, recommendations, and suggested portfolios for investors depending on their goals. Write to *The No-Load Investor,* P.O. Box 318, Irvingston-on-Hudson, NY 10533 (914-693-7420).

If you *really* are committed to learning about investing, consider the *Outstanding Investor Digest.* It is a quirky, thick newsletter that is published irregularly, costs a lot, and can run to 64 gray pages. That said, I must say that it is one of my favorites. I subscribed in December 1996 at a cost of $295, reduced from $495 because I agreed to an automatic credit card renewal.

I received my first 64-page issue in January, including lengthy interviews with investors like Michael Price of the Mutual Series funds and Ron Baron of Baron Asset. I have to admit it was daunting. But I read every word of how these experts pick stocks, what they look for in companies, how they invest. I figured I had to hurry and finish before the next issue came.

But I realized on June 4 that I had not yet received my second issue. I called to see if my name had been somehow lost. No, they said, the December issue was the latest one. I was told that a subscription covers 10 issues, rather than a calendar year.

I learned about *OID* from Don Phillips, president of *Morningstar Mutual Funds,* who told me it is one of the two publications that he reads immediately when he receives it. (The other is *Inside Information,* a newsletter for financial planners published by Robert N. Veres from Kennesaw, Georgia (770-424-8755, $95). Like other subscribers, Phillips reads *OID* to learn more about investing. It is for the hard core. And it's among the best.

There are lots of books on investing. Many of them require a commitment of several dozen hours to grapple with the principles. Not so with the books published by Bloomberg Press. Small-cap stocks were the investing story of 1997. And one of the best places to learn about them is *Investing in Small-Cap Stocks,* by Christopher Graja and Elizabeth Ungar (Bloomberg Press, 1997). I love this book. It is basic enough for the novice yet chock full of ideas that can help an intermediate investor learn more.

LIFESTYLE

THERE ARE PROBABLY LOTS of good lifestyle books out there. But many of them are too close to the motivational-speaker camp to be worthwhile. So just two books here. I received *Benjamin Franklin's The Art of Virtue: His Formula for Successful Living,* edited by George L. Rogers (Acorn Publishing, Eden Prairie, Minnesota, 1986), in the mail one day as a "thank you" for recommending the *Outstanding Investor Digest* to a number of friends who became subscribers. I found it to be a fascinating collection of Franklin's writing on everything from setting goals and objectives for your life to becoming a vegetarian to enjoying a productive old age.

I also like *Downshifting: Reinventing Success on a Slower Track,* by Amy Saltzman (Harper Collins, 1991; $19.95) for its inspiring stories of what can be done with a lot of enthusiasm and some ingenuity to create the life you want for yourself.

ON-LINE

BLOOMBERG ON-LINE (www.bloomberg.com) taps into the resources of Bloomberg Financial Markets, which are used by professionals in the financial world. The site also includes financial and world news, updated continuously, and features and columns from the monthly personal finance magazine, *Bloomberg Personal.*

The Morningstar Web site (www.morningstar.net) is worth a look. So is InvestorSquare (www.investor square.com), a site where you will find 9,500 funds that you can screen based on category.

Microsoft Investor (www.investor.msn.com) is an on-line magazine with weekly features and columns on the markets. Its younger sibling, *Money Insider* (www.moneyinsider.msn.com), provides personal finance basics that cover taxes, retirement, insurance, real estate. I write weekly columns for this site on investing, credit, and savings.

Anyone trying to figure out if the Roth IRA would be right for them should check out a great Web site (www.rothira.com) put together by Gregory Kolojeski, the tax attorney who runs Brentmark Software. It's quite thorough and contains links to lots of other calculators.

ABOUT BLOOMBERG

Bloomberg Financial Markets is a global, multi-media-based distributor of information services, combining news, data, and analysis for financial markets and businesses. Bloomberg carries real-time pricing, data, history, analytics, and electronic communications that are available 24 hours a day and are currently accessed by 250,000 financial professionals in 94 countries.

Bloomberg covers all key global securities markets, including equities, money markets, currencies, municipals, corporate/euro/sovereign bonds, commodities, mortgage-backed securities, derivative products, and governments. The company also delivers access to Bloomberg News, whose more than 540 reporters and editors in 80 bureaus worldwide provide around-the-clock coverage of economic, financial, and political events.

To learn more about Bloomberg—one of the world's fastest-growing real-time financial information networks—call a sales representative at:

Frankfurt:	49-69-920-410
Hong Kong:	852-2521-3000
London:	44-171-330-7500
New York:	1-212-318-2000
Princeton:	1-609-279-3000
San Francisco:	1-415-912-2960
São Paulo:	5511-3048-4500
Singapore:	65-226-3000
Sydney:	61-29-777-8686
Tokyo:	81-3-3201-8900

ABOUT THE AUTHOR

Mary Rowland is a distinguished columnist and author specializing in personal finance and financial planning issues. Her work has appeared in *The New York Times* and in *Bloomberg Personal, Dow Jones Investment Advisor, Modern Maturity,* and many other major magazines. For 20 years she has looked at financial planning from both sides, interviewing financial advisers and portfolio managers for professional journals and writing for consumers on such issues as selecting a financial planner. She is the author of *A Commonsense Guide to Mutual Funds* and *Best Practices for Financial Advisors,* and speaks frequently at industry conferences and investment seminars. She lives in New York's Hudson Valley with her husband and two children.